ƒP

Parents Under Siege

Why You Are the Solution,

Not the Problem,

in Your Child's Life

James Garbarino

Claire Bedard

The Free Press

New York   London   Toronto   Sydney   Singapore

$f\mathbf{P}$

THE FREE PRESS
A Division of Simon & Schuster, Inc.
1230 Avenue of the Americas
New York, NY 10020

For information about special discounts for bulk purchases,
please contact Simon & Schuster Special Sales:
1-800-456-6798 or business@simonandschuster.com
Designed by Karolina Harris
Manufactured in the United States of America
10   9   8   7   6   5   4   3   2   1
Library of Congress Cataloging-in-Publication Data
Garbarino, James.
Parents under siege: why you are the solution, not the problem,
in your child's life/James Garbarino, Claire Bedard.
p. cm.
Includes bibliographical references and index.
1. Parent and child. 2. Interpersonal relations. 3. Child rearing. I. Bedard, Claire.
II. Title.
HQ755.85 .G364 2001
649'.1—dc21   2001023692
ISBN 0-7432-0134-5

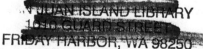

For Tom, Sue, and Byron Klebold
and for all the families
who have lost children

Contents

Preface

&o On April 20, 1999, the world of American parenting changed forever. At Columbine High School in Littleton, Colorado, two seniors—Eric Harris and Dylan Klebold—staged a lethal assault on their fellow students. After wounding more than a score of kids and killing twelve others and a teacher, the two boys killed themselves, ending the worst school massacre in American history. That day, as never before, parents learned that their kids could begin the day normally, as just kids going off on the bus, but end it shattered—physically or psychologically—or dead.

That day changed our lives. In an awful coincidence, my book *Lost Boys: Why Our Sons Turn Violent and How We Can Save Them* came out on April 20 and simultaneously arrived on the desks of journalists around the country. This propelled me, and my partner and social researcher, Claire Bedard, into the events in Littleton in a way we had not anticipated. For me, it meant weeks that stretched into months of nonstop interviews with journalists, on and off camera, offering my perspective as America struggled to make sense of these boys and their devastating violence. For Claire, it meant hearing from the scores of parents who called our home, wrote letters or e-mail, or reached her at her Cornell University office. A great many of the callers were mothers, who desperately wanted to share the fear they had until then silently carried around about the disturbing signs they were seeing in their own children, and who wondered if their sons could be the next school shooters.

Among the parents who contacted us in the months that followed were Tom and Sue Klebold. Yes, Dylan Klebold's parents. They had read *Lost Boys* in their own search for answers to what might have triggered what happened to their son. They were trying to understand the unfathomable: How could their seemingly normal, greatly beloved boy, turn out to be a mass murderer? Neither of them had reason to even imagine such a thing until after the massacre. The Klebolds were able to find some comfort in the book because it helped them see that they did not fit the typical pattern for families of lethally violent kids. This was a small consolation overall, but an emotionally important one for them as the surviving parents. But they were still left with only question marks when it came to explain what pattern, if any, could explain what had become of the son they thought they knew.

From the events in Littleton and from coming to know Dylan Klebold's parents, we developed a better appreciation for how and why "bad things happen to good parents." With the many interviews Claire and I had conducted for *Lost Boys* still fresh in our minds, we were deeply moved by what we were now observing about the dramatic challenges parents face today. And we came to a clearer appreciation of the not-always-obvious tools parents need to understand today's children and teenagers better—and to promote the development of character, empathy, patience, and all the other elements of what psychologist Daniel Goleman called "emotional intelligence."

We reflected upon our own experience as parents and what we knew from research on child development and parenting. We wrote this book to make sense of what we learned, to lay out our analysis in terms parents can relate to, and to set forth an approach to parenting that could help make things better. Our purpose had two steps. The first was to reach every parent, not just those at the extremes, but those dealing with the everyday challenges families face in these difficult times. Our second was to offer reassurance and guidance to families dealing with temperamentally vulnerable children and youth.

Parents Under Siege offers a psychological compass for finding a successful path through the cruel and perplexing dilemmas of being a twenty-first-century parent confronting perplexing child-rearing challenges. Of course we can never forget what happened in Littleton: the nightmare of just how terrible it can be when bad things happen to good parents.

Part One, "The Real Lives of Parents," explores the many hazards parents face in the modern world and finds answers to these challenges that lead to a positive path. Being more mindful of your own thoughts, feelings, and behavior leads to being a better observer of your child. You don't have to retreat to a monastery to do this, but you do need to engage in a practice of mindfulness that grounds your thoughts and actions in a spiritual foundation. Enlisting the support of social and spiritual resources outside the family leads to raising a more anchored child or teenager, one who can stand up against the dangerous temptations and dark side of American culture. Such resources empower parents to face the challenges that come from many sources.

Lately there has been a judgmental character in much of the public debate over American children and parents, one that usually assigns blame to parents. This is the topic of Chapter 1. Chapter 2 lays out a way of thinking about families and children that shifts our focus from who's to blame to a more scientifically grounded understanding of the parental role in the lives of children, and the limits of that role. Chapter 3 describes the many ways in which the stresses on modern families make it hard to cope with the difficult temperaments some children bring with them to family life. In Chapter 4 we tackle the tough parental assignment of helping children cope with the dangers of the world without incapacitating them with fear, cynicism, and despair. Finally, Chapter 5 examines the impulse many children and teenagers have to create secret lives unbeknownst to their parents, and the way the economic system encourages children to be little consumers. These challenges appear through the secret lives that youths create in modern pop culture through the Internet, television, movies, music, and video games.

Part Two is entitled "A Parent's Compass" because it offers parents a way to find and hold onto their personal "true north" on a daily basis. Here we present strategies to aid you in being a more positive influence in your child's life, first by finding the wellsprings of peace and harmony that reside within you (thus becoming a better observer of your own life), then by becoming a more mindful and observant parent, and by acting to improve your community.

These strategies grew out of a way of understanding human development that is grounded in the best research *and* in spiritual practice that enables parents to use time with children and teenagers more effectively. We don't make impossible or unrealistic demands of parents. We don't ask them to be superhuman. We only ask of them what we ask of ourselves—to be real and true to our highest selves, our deepest awareness of life's purpose, and to love.

Chapter 6 offers directions on how to succeed with temperamentally challenging children. In Chapter 7 we present ways to assert authority in a world that communicates and validates disrespect and anarchy in children and youth. Chapter 8 illuminates the path through the minefield of modern economic life, with its bombardment of messages and images of superficial, shallow materialism. Chapter 9 offers strategies for mastering the scary and degrading world of TV, video games, and the Internet. In an Epilogue, we think aloud about how success as a parent depends on being a good citizen outside the family, where some important decisions about the world in which children and parents must live are made. Finally, we offer a resource list for parents and professionals to use in following up in the long run.

We hope that when parents like us read this book they will

say, "Yes, this is what I've been looking for!" *Parents Under Siege* will leave them feeling calmer and more in control—first of themselves, and then of their child-rearing practices. By helping them to name their fears, we prepare them to master these fears. By showing them how to enter the secret lives of their children, we will open the way to finding positive paths for development, and knowing when and how to seek professional assistance in coping with children having special difficulties. We say all this with humility and empathy. We have been there, struggling to handle a difficult child, feeling besieged at home and unsure of ourselves as we sought to do the right thing. We don't judge or cast stones at parents because we know . . .

Parents Under Siege will equip parents to be better consumers of the thousands of books, magazines, television programs, and radio shows that offer them advice. It will free them to stop pretending we are living perfect lives. Accepting our imperfections is the starting point for a better family life. Why? Because it is the beginning of insight into what it means to be fully human and how to bring this insight to our children. It is the starting point for true parenting, true to our highest and deepest understanding of how and where human lives fit into the universe. For the authors, our roots in the Judeo-Christian tradition have been expanded and illuminated by our explorations of Buddhism—particularly the insights of Tibetan Buddhism as we have been introduced to it through the teachings of the Dalai Lama, in his books and in person.

We conducted interviews with parents specifically for this book, beginning with the Klebolds in Littleton, Colorado. Each chapter uses the lessons we learned to provide practical advice on how parents can respond to the problems they face, and what kind of help they may need from their communities and schools to do so.

Parents Under Siege includes challenges to parents from inside and outside the home. We address issues of social and cultural poisons in American life and how they affect children and youth. We pay special attention to temperamentally vulnerable and difficult children as well as those who fall into bad habits of challenging authority and straining parental patience to the breaking point. Second, we include a strong emphasis on spiritual issues without a specific and limiting religious sectarian orientation. The life of the spirit is vitally important to us, as it is to most parents. But it is often difficult for parents to see how their deepest connections to meaning in the universe translate into parenting practice. We have tried to make those translations.

We wrote this book because our way of looking at the whole picture of a parent-child relationship demands that we offer more than simply a recipe book. We put our faith in the science of human development, which insists that the meaning of specific child-rearing practices depends very much upon where, and when, and in what culture, and with which child we are parenting. Child-development research calls this *social context,* and assessing context is essential to acting wisely and effectively. In our academic training we learned to call this focus an *ecological perspective.* For example, several studies have shown the same childhood pattern of acting-out, aggression, disobedience, and violating the rights of others that leads to serious violent delinquency 60 percent of the time in one neighborhood leads to the same outcome in only 20 percent in another neighborhood.

Most how-to books assume parents can apply one set of rules and actions in any and every situation, with everyone, without regard to analyzing context. Do cookie-cutter strategies work for any parent? They certainly haven't worked for Claire and me as we've raised our own children—Josh, Joanna, and Eric. Instead, *Parents Under Siege* goes a step further than most books by offering guidance for parents to assess *their* situation and learn how to respond to the *specifics* of their situation.

Our essential lessons focus on:

- Why parents are responsible but not necessarily to blame when things go badly with their children.
- Why, to regain control, parents must first recognize the social forces surrounding their family today: excessively violent imagery and unsupervised access to video games and the Internet.
- How by paying careful attention to what is happening without judgment and preconceptions—what is called mindfulness—parents can see their children for who they are and appreciate how parental behavior contributes to the development of impossible children.
- How safety begins in the way children see the world, and thus teaching confidence rather than fear is the first responsibility of parents.
- That to establish their authority with their children, parents need to recognize and align themselves with the structures of adult authority in the world. Anarchy is not healthy for children.
- How parents can be in the same room with their child and yet be absent; the doorway to the secret lives of kids opens only to parents who listen without judgment before acting.
- Why being involved in formal religion is no guarantee for real parenting unless that religion offers a spiritual path based upon reverence for life, the universality of love, and a profound, nonjudgmental humility.
- How every difficult child has a positive path if only parents have the wisdom and community support to discover it and be with the child on that path.
- That wealth comes not from giving in to the commercial "pushers" who promise satisfaction through material acquisition, but only from a sense of personal connection to life's enduring values: love, the investment of energy, wisdom, joy, and affirmation.

Claire and I wrote this book *as* parents and *for* parents, with respect and humility. Being parents, we are humble about parenting—its challenges and its rewards. We don't talk down or water down ideas and concepts. We have made every effort to avoid oversimplifying things just to make our book appear easy; these are not easy matters to understand and deal with. Being a parent in twenty-first-century America is anything but simple. We know that from our professional work and from our experiences as parents—dealing with temperamentally complex children, with separation and divorce, with remarriage, and with the day-to-day exposure to media violence and commercialism that poisons children's minds and spirits. We are not about to throw stones at any parent because we know that in this complicated world, with these complicated children, and with all the inner turmoil in our own lives as adults, loving your kids is usually not the issue and often is not enough. We know that bad things happen to good parents and that many good parents feel besieged. The last thing any of us needs is more blame.

All this means that we speak with a voice of experience, and we hope with some authority. But most important, it means we speak with humility. Our imperfections as parents stimulate a deeply felt humility as we speak to other parents. We are aware that everything we say, everything we think we know, everything we do, is imperfect, shaped as it is by the specifics of time, place, and the personalities of our children.

Sitting with Tom and Sue Klebold and their remaining son, Byron, in their home in the wake of the Columbine High School shootings was more than enough to reinforce our profound humility. Here were two loving and intelligent parents, who cared for their two boys, who spent time with them, and looked after them, yet who had lost their second-born son. Dylan's picture appeared on the cover of *Time* magazine with the caption "MONSTER." Of all the parents we have met, the Klebolds were the quintessential "parents under siege." Their story was with us always as we went about writing this book. We dedicate it to them—and to Byron—as an act of kinship for a family battered by the slings and arrows of outrageous fortune.

Of course, in writing this book we leaned on many other people. We learned from the parents who were willing to "come out of the closet" and share their confusion, pain, frustration, and anger, as well as their yearning for success, their hopes and insights. We had help from our editor at The Free Press, Philip Rappaport, and our literary agent, Victoria Sanders. Each is our advocate in a special way. Two Cornell graduate students, Catherine Bradshaw and Joe Vorrasi, aided us in consolidating the references and the resource section. Lisa Rose helped with the mechanics of the manuscript. And we had the encouragement of the Family Life Development Center and of Patsy Brannon, Dean of the College of Human Ecology at Cornell University, where we make our academic home. And we thank our children, Josh, Joanna, and Eric, for hanging in there with us.

Part One

The Real Lives of Parents

1

When Bad Things Happen to Good Families

⁎ It all starts with compassion. You love your children. You want the best for them. You would give your life to save theirs. But sometimes love is not enough. Bad things happen to good families. Would you have compassion for a family in which a little girl died because she got into an unlocked medicine cabinet while her mom was on the phone? Would you feel compassion if a little boy were hit by a car while out riding his bike after his father had warned him many times not to ride in the street? To paraphrase Thich Nhat Hanh, the Zen master and peacemaker, compassion is not a principle, it is an energy in us waiting to manifest.

In the movie *Seven Years in Tibet*, there is an unforgettable scene in which Heinrich Harrer, played by Brad Pitt, is asked to build a movie house for the young Dalai Lama, at the Potala Palace, in Lhasa, Tibet. As the excavation begins, Heinrich arrives at the site and is greeted by a group of monks rushing toward him, looking absolutely frantic. They gesture toward the ground and implore the unsuspecting Heinrich to stop all digging; they explain that the worms hiding in the earth are being trampled and destroyed. Stunned by their concern for even these lives, Heinrich is left speechless.

He returns to see his friend, the young Dalai Lama, who explains to him that Tibetans believe that all living beings are to be protected against harm and suffering. This compassion is at the core of their spiritual practice and beliefs as Buddhists. When Heinrich protests that such compassion is impractical, the Dalai Lama reassures him, confident that he will find a creative solution to the problem.

The next scene reveals the solution. The monks kneel on the ground in two rows: one row of monks digs and places the mounds of dirt into bags, while the second row goes through the bags, gently removing each worm and placing it in a bowl for transportation to another environment where the worms can continue to live happily and fulfill their purpose. Why is this so important to us? Because it is a true story. This scene is not some movie fantasy, but rather a true portrait of Tibetan Buddhist belief and an accurate reflection of a people's nonviolence and respect for all living beings, great or small. For the Dalai Lama, it all starts with compassion.

Decades later, the adult Dalai Lama says of compassion: True compassion is not just an emotional response, but a firm commitment founded on reason. Therefore, a truly compassionate attitude toward others does not change, even if they behave negatively. Through universal altruism you develop a feeling of responsibility for others, the wish to actively help them overcome their problems.

In the summer of 2000 we spent a week listening to the 65-

year-old Dalai Lama teach compassion. We were fortunate enough to have an audience with him, along with 200 other Americans, and we recommitted ourselves to living lives of compassion. The goal of this chapter—indeed, of the whole book—is to bring this commitment to parenting. So, following the counsel of the Dalai Lama, we begin with the process of understanding, which is the most reliable foundation for compassion. We want you to know why and how parents are under siege—why maybe you are under siege—and encourage you to use understanding to act with compassion, with your own children, with other parents, with yourself.

The challenges parents face exist on a spectrum. At one end are the day-to-day issues—for example, getting infants to sleep through the night, toilet training toddlers, getting first-graders to pick up their toys, ensuring that sixth-graders do their homework, and making sure teenagers don't drink and drive. At the other end are the frightening problems that confront a minority of parents—an infant with spina bifida, a child with cancer, a teenager who is paralyzed in a car accident. But certain difficulties require even more compassion than the child damaged physically through chance, some genetic defect or some lurking virus, or some random danger: Some children seem to volunteer for trouble, resisting everyone who tries to help and guide them toward a positive path.

Anything Can Happen

In Chicago, a mother walked her 7-year-old son, Dantrell, to school every morning. Their inner city neighborhood was a dangerous place to walk alone, and she always feared for his safety. One day in 1992, she accompanied Dantrell to school, and as the daily ritual goes, she let go of his hand to let him walk the last 75 feet to the front door, where teachers were standing on the steps to greet him. As usual, cops were sitting in a parked car at the corner. But this time, as he walked toward the school, a shot rang out and Dantrell fell dead, shot in the head by a gang member out to revenge himself against an opponent's little boy. It happened in broad daylight, in everyone's sight.

Seven years later, on April 20, 1999, a mother in the affluent Denver suburb of Littleton, Colorado, watched her beloved son get on the school bus to Columbine High School. Content in her knowledge that the day would unfold with the same predictability only such a small, affluent community enclave can provide these days, she went on with the rest of her day. Such peace of mind was, after all, why they had moved to this area. A security guard was stationed at the school, and surveillance cameras protected the building. A few hours later she learned from television reports that her son was dead, shot in the head by two of his classmates.

Anything can happen. This is the lesson American parents have taken with them into the twenty-first century, the one that resonates the loudest and ultimately leaves no parent unaffected. This is a parent's "Vietnam," the strange war that happens in faraway places and then suddenly hits home. It has profoundly affected the way parents think about other people's children and their own. Like the Vietnam lesson of the 1960s and 1970s, the anything-can-happen lesson of Littleton, Colorado, is part of our national consciousness. We want this terror to go away, yet it won't completely disappear.

For some of us it is a whispering voice inside; for others it is full-blown terror. Parents are uncomfortable with the status quo. The discomfort is hard to articulate for most, but undeniable. Not everyone's eyes are open, though when it is your child who is in trouble, you see it clearly. A mother tells us this. "My husband and I have given everything we have to being good parents, and our son is only getting into deeper trouble. We don't know where to turn anymore, and all we get is 'What are you doing wrong?' Not in so many words, but in the way some other parents look at us, or in the comments they make." Parents sleep better at night believing that if only they do things right, they are guaranteed good outcomes. Thus they resist compassion. They resist empathy. They yearn to believe they are immune. It's an understandable impulse. But the more you know, the more you know you must resist it.

In September 2000 we were participating in a program with Frank DeAngelis, the principal of Columbine High School. The moderator asked him what he had learned from all that had happened. He replied that if someone had asked him on April *19*, 1999, if it was possible there were boys in his school so angry and troubled that they were planning to destroy the school, he would have said, "Impossible." But what he learned on April *20*, 1999, was that it was possible, that it is possible anywhere in our country. Ask any American parent who has looked with open eyes, without the comfort of denial.

"If I work hard as a parent, my children will turn out okay." That is the unspoken guarantee of the American Dream of Parenting. We are told that you get back what you put in, a guiding principle that has sustained parents for generations because it seemed logical, and it seemed to work for most of us, most of the time. It made sense. It offered direction, order, and predictability to our ongoing efforts to make something of our children. It promised a reward at the end of a job well done. Some among us still believe it.

After one of Jim's lectures in the weeks after the Columbine High School shootings, a school board member in a small town in New York State stood up and said indignantly, "It couldn't happen in my family! Not with my kids! Not in my school!" We wish he were right. Frank DeAngelis would have agreed—until the day it happened in his school. So would Dylan Klebold's parents—until the day it happened to their family.

The 1990s threatened the American Dream of Parenting as never before. The problems surrounding our children and youth became increasingly more serious: rising suicide rates, drug abuse, explosive youth crime, and increasing rates of depression in young people. In 1999 *USA Today* asked American parents to comment on the difficulty of being a parent then compared with twenty years ago—specifically, whether parents thought it was more difficult to raise children to be "good people." Almost 90 percent answered "Yes." Three out of four indicated that materialism and the negative influences of pop culture and the mass media were a "serious problem" in trying to raise good children.

No single event brought this home more than the school shootings committed by Dylan Klebold and his friend Eric Harris in Littleton. While we don't know Eric's parents, we know Dylan's parents, and we can assert without a doubt that they are good parents—attentive, involved, and loving. Yet Dylan still developed a bizarre rage against humanity that he and Eric documented in a series of chilling home videotapes made in the months before their attack on their school. We know Dylan's parents are good parents, and still he reached the point where he planned and implemented the massacre of his schoolmates. The shooting left a dozen kids dead, and their parents in shock that this could happen. While their story is extreme, many good parents have discovered that their children are not who they think they were.

Listen to one mother's account.

I remember having had some concerns about Christopher when he was little, and again in Grade 5 when he was caught stealing something at the corner store, one aisle away from where I stood. Toward the end of grade school, his teachers also started complaining about how he was acting-out in class. We took him to a psychologist for testing, and he concluded that Christopher had mild Attention Deficit Disorder. We had never considered such a thing until then, and we were not particularly knowledgeable about ADD. We thought that although Christopher could be hyperactive at times, he could also be super-engrossed in activities. He could be very focused. However, as I began to read about ADD and ADHD, the description of the syndrome seemed to fit so many things in Christopher that we accepted the diagnosis. At the time, the therapist said it was not something that required therapy or medication. He did warn us that things might become worse, because as they become more academically challenged, there will be problems. He left the option of treatment open as a possibility in the future. The psychologist also relieved us of guilt and the great feeling of responsibility my husband and I felt regarding Christopher's behavior. Some of the impulsive behaviors he engaged in didn't make sense to us, and I actually thought there was something we had failed to teach him. I think when he was shoplifting in the next aisle, I took it as a moral failure on our part, and I do have to admit that one day I had him write all Ten Commandments at the kitchen table. But the psychologist said that all the Ten Commandments in the world are not going to change an impulsive type of decision making, and if you love him you hang in with him but be prepared that there will be difficult times. It isn't a moral problem, it is an issue of impulsiveness and unpredictability. The therapist was right. Things did become difficult. Christopher became a habitual truant, and we eventually found out that he was using drugs, probably more than we will ever really know. He disengaged more and more from our family and started spending the night away, then several nights at a time. We would call all his friends, at least the ones we knew of, and often could not find him until he came home on his own. Devastated as we were, we continued to hope.

The promise of getting back what you put in doesn't seem like such a sure thing. Growing numbers of American parents have come to realize that things have changed. To be sure, some of us hang on to the old comforting rationalizations. A mother in Mississippi tells us, "I still insist that if you are blameless, nothing bad can happen." But more and more parents look at what is happening to families like the Klebolds' and say to themselves, "I think I've been a good parent—but what happened to them could happen to me." Parents are afraid and confused, bombarded with contradictory advice from the Right and the Left, blamed if their children turn out screwed up, and swinging between hysterical overreaction and numbed resignation. Parents need compassion, based on understanding.

But Do the Issues Ever Really Change?

The philosopher George Santayana wrote, "Those who cannot remember the past are condemned to repeat it." Many Americans are unwilling to look at history in more than a casual way, but when it comes to understanding parenting, we need to start with history. Ten years ago Jim was asked to deliver an address on the occasion of the hundredth anniversary of the founding of a family service association in Chicago. The topic was to be the challenges parents and families would face in the coming millennium. To prepare himself for that assignment, Jim sat in a public park that had been in operation for 100 years and read over some old newspapers from the 1890s. The exercise was illuminating. The issues for parents and families as the twentieth century dawned were these, among others:

1. Substance abuse (opium) and addiction (alcohol) were recognized as insidious and powerfully destructive forces in family life.
2. There was evidence of a widening gap between rich and poor, and many voices called for action to improve the conditions of the poor—particularly the "worthy" poor, what we today would call the "working poor."

3. Traditional American values and institutions were being challenged by the influx of immigrants who did not speak English, were perceived as making disproportionate demands on social services, and who were suppressing wages by accepting low pay, long hours, and inferior working conditions.
4. The legacy of slavery and the reality of racism lurked behind the public facade of democracy and broke out in dramatic incidents of lynching and race riots from time to time.
5. To their contemporaries, growing numbers of girls and women appeared to be in moral jeopardy due to the frequency of premarital sex and pregnancy; and the sex industry flourished.
6. Child abuse was entering the public consciousness, and there was a sense that juvenile crime was escalating.
7. Significant numbers of families were not intact, as mothers frequently died in childbirth and fathers often abandoned families.

Does this sound familiar?

The French have a saying that translates as "The more things change, the more they remain the same." There have been changes in the past hundred years, of course: divorce and unmarried-teen births have replaced maternal death and paternal separation as the main causes of "incomplete" families; openly gay and lesbian adults now publicly claim the right to be parents; more women combine employment and motherhood; and scientific and public understanding of child abuse as a social problem has increased. Looking back even thirty or forty years to our own childhood, we can see these changes coming. But all this is nothing compared to what parents are facing today.

Most adults recognize that things have changed in the last decade when it comes to children. A survey conducted in 1997 for the Gannett News Service revealed that "adults have a very pessimistic view of children's lives." In comparison to when they were children, 79 percent of adults said they thought children live in less stable homes, 75 percent said they thought children are growing up in less safe neighborhoods, 64 percent said children have poorer role models, and 50 percent said they thought children are less happy today than they themselves were as children.

But in our efforts to understand the rapidly changing situation of parents and children, let us not forget that some of the dilemmas we face have deeper roots in the American experience. After all, it was as we entered the *twentieth* century that some of the major themes in public debates about parenting were laid down: the costs and benefits of industrialization and a global economy; multiculturalism; "big government"; a human rights perspective on racism; militarism and empire; the emergence of mass media; and a search for *the* ideal American family.

In 1900 the United States was being transformed by the seemingly unstoppable power of industrialism and was becoming a major player in the global economy. These changes had massive implications for families. New economic relationships emerged between husbands and wives, and young girls became independent economic entities as they entered the cash economy. The look of America changed dramatically as we started full scale the process of giving everything a dollar price in the economy (moving activities from what an economist would call the "nonmonetarized" to the "monetarized" economies). For example, child care first emerged as a job with a salary, and today it is a multibillion-dollar-a-year industry. And as America moved from an agrarian to an urban society, a new residential form emerged: the suburb.

It was then, a hundred years ago, that progressive leaders like President Theodore Roosevelt began to believe that "big government" was required as a counterforce to "big business" if the best of America's commitment to human rights was to be preserved. As private industrial and financial entities grew, they began to achieve a political power outside the scope envisioned by the Founding Fathers. This stimulated a constitutional crisis. On one side was our traditional belief in small government and a narrow interpretation of the Constitution. On the other stood the need to grow the federal government to preserve the people's rights to life, liberty, and the pursuit of happiness amid the complexities of a modern industrial society. This conflict led the Franklin Roosevelt administration to throw the weight of the national government behind efforts to end the Great Depression, and the conflict has continued to this very day.

The year 1900 saw the initial creation of Imperial America, the America of the military-industrial complex, projecting power globally and putting forward commercial markets as the basis for foreign policy. At the same time, America was challenged to refine the meaning of its identity as an Anglo culture. De facto bilingualism in schools and neighborhoods contested with a strong prejudice favoring English-speaking Americans, who saw themselves as the *real* Americans. This was, of course, ironic, since truly *Native* Americans were excluded from this culture. All these events were taking place in the context of what historian Frederick Jackson Turner had described in 1897 as "the closing of the American frontier." Free access to open public lands in the West—which had served as a pressure valve for American society by allowing the disaffected to move rather than deal with conflict—was ending. Thus began the process of confronting rather than simply displacing social issues that continues to this day.

Finally, the rise of a mass media created a force to shape a truly national consciousness and perhaps a collective *unconscious* formed by the implicit images that permeate the shared experience of those who read, listen to, and watch the same material. Current analyses of television and movies and homogenizing cultural forces have parallels a century ago, when American families could partake of a national experience of fashion, music, and important events.

Much more could be said about the late nineteenth century and its relevance to understanding our approach to parenting in the twenty-first. Our responses to challenging historical events have always reflected some deeply rooted themes in American culture. These themes mattered then; they matter now. Understanding the specifics of parenting requires that we understand the context in which we raise the questions and provide the answers.

How and when families are private and how and when they are public are key questions at the heart of many parenting issues. How far can parents go in doing what they want with their children? How far can government go in setting limits and enforcing them?

Are children first and foremost citizens, with a direct relationship with society, or private members of families, or the private property of parents? Americans tend to see families as the primary unit of society, and the state having authority only as a last resort. Some societies (such as the Puritans of colonial New England in the seventeenth and eighteenth centuries) see parents as the agent of God; others define parenting as a purely secular matter. Some societies define parents as child-rearing agents of society, as did the former Soviet Union. These are important distinctions.

Today, the United States is one of only a tiny number of countries that has not ratified the United Nations Convention on the Rights of the Child. Why? Among several reasons is a well-organized and well-financed campaign to defeat the Convention because of its perceived threat to parental autonomy and power, and its general opposition to using physical force against children (including a prohibition against the death penalty being applied to teenagers).

The more we see the child as a part of society, not just the family, the more we are likely to regard conceiving a child as tantamount to entering into a contract with the community. The social-contract approach provides a moral basis for public efforts to ensure the safety and quality of the resulting child, since a contract implies mutual obligations and rights. The opposing vision portrays the relationship between families and society as voluntary and entirely up to the parents.

Today's public debates about families reflect these basic differences. They show up in discussions about child welfare (is it an entitlement? a privilege? a tool for social control?), about teen pregnancy (who has authority over a girl who gets pregnant?), and about divorce and child support (is financial responsibility for a child part of the private contract between divorced adults, or is it a public responsibility?).

And more and more it shows up in debates over parents' accountability when their kids commit antisocial acts. The parents of Dylan Klebold and Eric Harris were sued for $300 million by their victims' families, who charged them with being negligent to have failed to see what was happening with their sons and intervene effectively. As we write this, the claims have been settled for about $2 million.

Raising Children in a World Full of Social and Cultural Poisons

It's not easy being a parent. How many times a week does this thought dance through your head? But lurking around the edges of this common awareness is every parent's worst nightmare: that something terrible and beyond your control will happen to your child. Some of the challenges parents face have plagued them for generations: understanding temperamentally difficult children, disciplining without breaking the child's spirit, teaching confidence and bravery in unsafe neighborhoods, and dealing with economic hardship. At the same time, parenting always takes place in a particular time, place, and culture—what many social scientists would call the social environment or context.

In our work we often refer to the culture of North America as socially toxic. Just as the physical environment we live in can become contaminated by the presence of lead, PCBs or radioactivity, social contaminants can become hazardous to our emotional and psychological health. The peril to our youth rises in the presence of violence-saturated media and a base exploitation of children through predatory advertising that stimulates or overstimulates cravings for specific snacks or toys—often unhealthy sweets and games without any redeeming character-building effects.

Let's consider the various challenges that have emerged over the last few decades, the kind that can try any parent's soul and resolve:

- Managing our children's access to the Internet, where even doing one's homework can lead to such nastiness as researching the White House for a fifth-grade social studies assignment and ending up in a pornographic Web site named Whitehouse.com.
- Evaluating the seriousness of children's TV viewing (leaving children alone to watch TV, even during the day or early evening, can expose them to material that is viciously degrading).
- Constantly responding to children who are in league with advertisers whose main interest in them is as consumers, and who are shameless in exploiting their naïveté (a shopping trip to the mall can be like running the gauntlet when every store displays some attempt by marketers to develop new and younger consumers of their products).

- Coping with the widespread availability of illicit drugs more powerful and deadly than our generation ever experienced. (Try to explain to a 14-year-old that the marijuana available to him is many times stronger than that with which our generation's college students could experiment.)
- Maintaining authority in the face of relentless media portrayals of parents as either bumbling or vicious (like the movies and television shows in which the only people who seem to know what they are doing is the kids, often in stark contrast to their troubled and dysfunctional parents).
- Developing spiritual values in a culture that hammers home the message that our self-worth depends on the cars we drive, the clothes we wear, and the ski resort, private island, or ranch where we last vacationed.
- Dealing with the threat of guns and bombs being used against children and teenagers in schools and the community.

All adults who care about children grapple with these poisonous influences, regardless of income, race, and social status, or whether they live in urban neighborhoods, in the suburbs, and in small cities, towns, and hamlets in rural areas. What is more, in this toxic social environment, the *costs of failure* are greater than ever, the challenges more daunting. We see that in the lives of the most affected: kids who kill.

What Lessons Can We Learn from Kids Who Kill?

Perhaps no issue highlights the controversy over parental responsibility as much as assessing blame when teenagers commit murder. In the days after the Littleton shootings, it was natural for anyone to wonder, How could those parents not have known that their sons were collecting guns and building bombs? How could they not have seen how troubled and angry those two boys were?

Boys commit about 85 percent of all youth homicides, and there are two pathways that lead to lethal youth violence. The first—which accounts for about 90 percent of the cases—conforms to a predictable pattern in which the line from "bad parenting" and "bad environments" to murder is usually clear. Their cases rarely make the national news, and in our work we see these boys and young men in the courtroom, in prison, and on death row with depressing regularity. We wrote about such unfortunate youngsters in *Lost Boys*. Their home life is often characterized by physical abuse, emotional deprivation and neglect, rejection, abandonment, and inadequate guidance. They face threats from the world outside their door—neglected neighborhoods, the illicit drug economy, the gang culture, and often the added trauma of racism. Put all this together, and it is not surprising that in a violent society like ours these damaged children become lethally violent teenagers.

But what about the other 10 percent of kids who kill, the boys who have not been abused, who have loving parents, who are not poor, and who have not been on the receiving end of social deprivation? What about affluent and loved boys like Dylan Klebold and Eric Harris in Littleton, or Kip Kinkel in Springfield, Oregon? What about boys who come from "good homes," yet still take the pathway that leads to murder? Are parents to blame when *these* kids become killers? What we have learned is that the answer is no. Here's why.

Most children are robust and resilient, but some children are fragile. Good parenting may not be enough to protect fragile children and ensure their healthy development. Swedish psychiatrist Barbro Lundquist sees it this way. Some children are like dandelions: they thrive if given only half a chance. Others are more like orchids: they do fine while they are young enough to be sheltered and nurtured by loving parents, but wilt when they enter adolescence and are thrown to the wolves of peer competition, bullying, and rejection, particularly in big high schools. Research shows that while only 10 percent of children who are born temperamentally "easy" have adjustment problems in elementary school, 70 percent of those who are temperamentally "difficult" have such problems. And, while many young children who are fragile do fine in early childhood, 50 percent have significant difficulties once they enter adolescence.

Parents are not the only influence. Beyond the front door, children respond to the powerful effects of their peers, their community, and the larger culture. Psychologists Rolf Loeber and David Farrington report that while in some communities only 20 percent of seriously troubled and aggressive 10-year-olds become chronically violent teenage delinquents, in other communities the figure is 50 percent or more. And the link between being a troubled teenager and committing murder is much stronger in American society than it is in others. For example, at the height of the murder epidemic during the mid-1990s, the youth homicide rate in the United States was about ten times higher than in Canada, due in large part to the use of guns by troubled teenagers. It remains much higher today.

Today's "normal" adolescent culture contains elements that are so twisted, degraded, vicious and dark that it becomes harder and harder for parents (and professionals) to distinguish between what in a youth's talk, dress, and taste in music, films, and video games indicates psychological trouble and what is simply a sign of the times. And these influences are being felt by younger and younger kids. Preteens as young as 8 are often steeped in that culture. For example, most kids who subscribe to the trench-coated Goth lifestyle, or who have multiple body piercings or who spend time listening to Marilyn Manson and play video games like Doom and Resident Evil 2, are just emotionally normal kids caught up in the pop culture of the day. It is often extremely difficult to figure out if a kid is just a chameleon changing colors to fit in with his peers by looking and sounding like what MTV says is cool, or if his attachment to the dark culture is a way of expressing his internal troubles. And the task becomes all the more difficult because it *is* more common for kids to be seriously troubled today than even twenty-five years ago.

In the mid-1970s, 10 percent of our kids were troubled enough to require professional mental health services; today the figure is about 20 percent. What is more, the very love parents have for their children may blind them to their dark side. How many parents can truly think the worst of their child? Where do we find the fortitude to imagine our son may be harboring murderous fantasies and might go as far as acting them out, or that our daughter takes part in a sex ring that engages in weekly orgies? In the real world of parenting today, parents have *had* to come to know this about their kids.

Here's what one mother told us:

> I never knew my daughter was involved in all these problems until I had to identify her at the morgue. Then I found out she had been selling drugs and spending a lot of her time with other kids who use drugs. I believed her when she told me she was just "hanging out," thinking that is what teens do. She was fine at home: she did her homework, she did her chores. She kept to herself a lot, but we thought that was normal. They told me she died from taking laced ecstasy. We didn't even know what ecstasy was. We thought things were going fine until that phone call that turned our lives into hell. We had no idea.

Many troubled kids develop secret lives, and parents often don't have all the information they need to know what is going on. Intelligent kids with good social skills and plenty of resources can be very good at hiding who they really are from their parents. They may do this to avoid punishment, to escape the shame of being identified as "crazy," or to protect the parents they love from being disappointed or worried. For example, in the wake of the shooting rampage that took the lives of his parents and schoolmates in Springfield, Oregon, Kip Kinkel confessed that he had been hearing voices but didn't tell anyone. Dylan Klebold successfully hid his inner turmoil from his loving parents. He put up a false front of normality—for example, visiting campuses in anticipation of starting college—at the very time that he and Eric were planning their deadly assault on Columbine High School and their own suicides. The shame and stigma of mental illness is still so strong that most kids, especially boys, cannot bear to admit to themselves or to their loving, concerned parents how troubled they really are.

Peer influence produces situations in which two kids will do what one would not do alone. This means that even if parents know their child as an individual, they may not (perhaps *cannot*) understand what that child is capable of when in the company of another child. Truman Capote described this in his classic book *In Cold Blood,* when he concluded that neither of the young men who massacred a family in Kansas would have committed that act on his own, but that together they produced a lethal synchronicity. From what we know, it appears that Dylan Klebold was not a killer on his own. It took his relationship with Eric Harris to make it happen. When *The New York Times* investigated cases of mass murder in the United States going back over many decades, they found one thing that differentiated those committed by teenagers from murders committed by adults. The adults were all isolated loners, while the teenagers acted with peer support.

In cases where parents abuse, reject, neglect, abandon, terrorize, and ignore their children, at least the link between

parental behavior and the murders their children commit seems clearer. But what if parents love, nurture, and generally look after their kids? Then, we think, we must refrain from blaming and judging. Bad things do happen to good people.

Even good parents can lose their children if those children are temperamentally vulnerable, develop a secret life of distorted thinking and troubled emotions, get caught up in the dark side of the culture, and form dangerous peer alliances in person or through the Internet. This may be frightening to acknowledge, but it's the starting point of our explanation of parents under siege, rearing difficult children in a difficult society.

Blaming Never Helps. Only Understanding Heals.

Shared responsibility and understanding hold the seeds of progress toward relieving parents under siege. Our spiritual beliefs, our experience as parents, and our academic research convince us that blaming never helps. Rather than simplistically pointing the finger at parents—and offering parent responsibility legislation, as others have done—we offer a realistic and sympathetic look at parenting in today's world. We recognize that parents are often frustrated when they seek help for their troubled children and teenagers. Simply lecturing parents on the need for responsibility or threatening them with penalties if things go badly will not work. It is essential that we embrace the idea that parents are responsible, but not to blame, if we are to get real about parents and parenting in the twenty-first century.

In *Seven Years in Tibet,* when the Dalai Lama was alerted by the Tibetan monks that worms were vulnerable to the damage that digging was doing to their environment, his response was not "It's their own fault." Or "Only the strong survive." Or "Blame it on the worms' parents." Instead, the whole community of monks acted with compassion and gave the worms what they needed: protection from harm and help in finding a safer environment. Lucky for the worms they were not parents and their children living in America.

Lesson: Compassion based upon understanding is the starting point for relieving parents under siege and helping kids grow toward health and the virtues of character they need for a successful life.

2

A Compassionate Look at Parental Responsibility

&o Popular movies often capture important themes in our culture. In the film *Reservoir Dogs,* actor Harvey Keitel created a powerful image of his character, a blazing weapon in each hand, brutally shooting down two police officers. Some viewers may have dismissed this image as pure fantasy. But to others it came to symbolize righteous revenge, as it did to Dylan Klebold, who wore this image on a T-shirt for his high school photo.

After the Columbine shootings, many people in the movie industry were asked to comment on the role of violence in fiction versus violence in reality. Harvey Keitel was quoted as saying, "If someone focuses on my image on that T-shirt, they are again avoiding the central issue here: Where have the *parents* failed?" He added: "After the shootings, I called my daughter and asked her 'Sweetheart, I need you to help me understand where we are going wrong as parents.'"

Keitel was not alone blaming parents exclusively. In the weeks and months after the massacre, the country rang with renewed calls for parental responsibility, for better parenting, and for more discipline and supervision. For example, an article in the May 17, 1999, issue of *U.S. News & World Report* was entitled "Who's Guilty: Parents are being sued and jailed for their children's sins." It outlined the many ways in which "parental responsibility" is making itself felt as a driving concept in law, litigation, and popular culture. The trend is for courts to hold parents morally and financially liable for what their kids do. But as we see it, more and more good parents are finding that their influence seems limited, and more bad things are happening to good families. Our goal in this chapter is to address this issue with tough-minded analysis *and* compassion, to look clearly at the issue of parental responsibility, but to do so with a compassion born of understanding.

This mother speaks for millions of others when she tells us: "My husband and I have given everything we have to being good parents, and our son is only getting into deeper trouble. We don't know where to turn anymore, and all we get is 'What are you doing wrong?' Not in so many words, but in the way some other parents look at us, or in the comments they make."

Parents are responsible, but not necessarily to blame. This is not just our opinion, but a fact. Parents are responsible for their children as a matter of law, until and unless they give up that responsibility or have it taken away by the courts. Some 44,000 children each year in the United States are caught up in legal proceedings that terminate the custody of their parents. The most likely cause is chronic or severe child abuse and neglect that leads to involuntary termination of parental rights. Many thousands more parents temporarily lose custody when their children are placed in foster care.

Millions of other families enter the court system voluntarily each year to deal with custody issues arising from separation and divorce. And, states and communities around the country have parental responsibility laws that hold parents legally and often financially accountable for the acts of their children—for example, judgments forcing parents to pay restitution for the delinquent acts of their underage children. But there is another face to the issue of parental responsibility—that of parental influence. How do parents influence the development of their children? Developmental psychologists ask, "Are parents the cause of their child's behavior?"

Judith Harris received national attention in 1998 with the publication of her book *The Nurture Assumption*, in which she argued that parental actions don't matter much in how children turn out, compared with biological and peer influences. We don't entirely agree. We have read many studies demonstrating that what parents do with and to their children does matter. The effects are usually not as simple and direct as many would like to believe, but they are there. The essential point we would like readers to keep in mind is that the child development equation includes a constantly shifting and evolving interplay of the child's biology and the parents' actions, and both are influenced by other children and adults, culture, institutions, and history. The success or failure of parenting depends in large part upon the difficulties posed by the children and by the degree to which the social environment is toxic and hostile to children and parents, as opposed to healthy and supportive.

For example, a study published in 1978 by Swedish psychologist Michael Bohman examined the fate of adopted children who had at least one biological parent with a criminal record. The underlying question was whether or not any biological predisposition to antisocial behavior these children may have inherited would predispose them to repeat the pattern of criminality in the next generation. And indeed, these children *were* more likely themselves to end up with a criminal record than children without such a heritage. However, the odds of repeating their biological parents' pattern depended greatly upon the kinds of families into which they were adopted.

When these children were adopted into high-risk families, 40 percent ended up with criminal records. But when adopted into well-functioning families, only 12 percent repeated the problem. Same kids, different outcomes. In the high-risk families, the likelihood that the children would repeat their biological family's pattern of criminality increased threefold. Nonetheless, the 12-percent rate in the well-functioning families was well above the average for other kids in well-functioning families, about 3 percent.

Blaming parents and demanding more parental responsibility may make some people feel more secure in their righteousness, but it misses the real point. In matters of human development, when the question is "Does X cause Y?" the best scientific answer is "It depends." Parents don't parent in isolation. Parenting depends upon the social context in which it occurs. Understanding this as more than a surface generality requires that we each employ a kind of "conceptual toolbox" to explore parenting in depth.

People often say that being a parent is the hardest job any of us will ever have. But while many important adult activities require a license—driving a car, for example—parenting does not. Moreover, few of us are fully prepared for the job, and rely on on-the-job training after our first child arrives. As parents, we are at a disadvantage compared with other jobs we hold. Many jobs depend on having the correct tools available. Like most families, we have in our kitchen a drawer known to all as "the tool drawer," which contains the tools required to keep the household running smoothly—for example, a hammer, several screwdrivers, work gloves, a drill, and pliers. Each has a function; some have multiple uses.

The nineteenth-century writer Mark Twain is credited with the aphorism, "If the only tool you have is a hammer, you tend to approach every problem as if it were a nail." This point is well taken, as is the reverse: "If you define every problem as a nail, the only tool you look for is a hammer." Both versions are useful reminders, and indicate why so much of the advice that experts offer to parents is misleading.

In October 2000, *Newsweek* magazine addressed this in an article entitled "The Real Parenting Expert Is . . . You." The article speaks eloquently about the fact that experts are often in conflict with each other—and leave parents feeling confused, frustrated, and abused. There are thousands of advice books and magazine articles, but no consensus. As the author, Heidi Murkoff, points out, there is more knowledge about child rearing than ever before.

> But too much information can have the opposite effect. Instead of building parental confidence, it can tear it down. Instead of empowering parents, it can render them impotent and ineffective. Instead of helping parents figure out the best routes to raising a child well, it can leave them bewildered, overwhelmed, uncertain how to proceed—paralyzed. Too much information can also suffocate a parent's instincts, stifling that small, smart voice within us all that tells us what's right for our child.

In an article published in the July 26, 1999, issue of *The New Yorker*, Hendrik Hertzberg takes the parental advice industry to task for being alarmist, and for undermining the confidence of parents. He speaks with disdain of the plethora of magazines that purport to inform and guide parents, ridiculing "the idea that a magazine produced by strangers in a distant city could help people bring up their children." His skepticism about the validity and usefulness of expert advice on parenting is understandable.

Cornell University psychologists Wendy Williams and Stephen Ceci address this issue in a more rigorous way in their book *Escaping the Advice Trap*. Williams and Ceci posed a series of common problems in family relations, child rearing, and interpersonal relationships to a group of experts to find out how similar their advice would be. They found that in many cases the experts came up with diametrically opposed advice: Expert number 1 says "Do this; don't do that," while Expert number 2 says "Do that; don't do this." At the heart of their analysis is that "despite the fact that experts may disagree on specifically what to do, they often agree on the most important factors in the situation." When Williams and Ceci looked at the reasons for the discrepancies, they found several themes, which they describe in The Twelve Golden Rules of Personal Decision Making.

Among them are: "There are two or more sides to every story." "Always seek a second (or third) opinion." And "If you're too close to a problem, it can be difficult to see a solution." One of the messages from their research is that we need a variety of tools to figure out what is going on with kids and then do something about it. It is in that spirit that we offer ten items in our parenting toolbox, which go far beyond the kitchen toolbox. They include a variety of intellectual tools, ideas and concepts that we can bring to bear in the complex task of parenting in the twenty-first century. Put together, these tools are what parents need to become more acutely aware, more mindful, and more effective in dealing with growing children and adolescents.

- Tool 1: An Intellectual Microscope for Looking at the World of Children
- Tool 2: A Periscope for Seeing the World Through the Eyes of Each Child's Individual Temperament
- Tool 3: A Spiritual Fulcrum for Moving the Child to a Positive Place

- Tool 4: A Developmental Calculator for Tallying Up the Accumulation of Risks and Opportunities in a Child's Life
- Tool 5: The Glue Stick of Resilience for Holding Together a Child's World in Difficult Times
- Tool 6: A Psychological Tape Measure for Mapping a Child's World
- Tool 7: A Social Geiger Counter for Isolating Cultural Poisons in the Child's Experience
- Tool 8: The Moral Compass of Character
- Tool 9: A Psychological Jack for Supporting Children as They Build Character and Competence
- Tool 10: A Set of Multicultural Keys for Unlocking Cultural Resources to Meet a Child's Social Challenges

These are the ten conceptual tools parents need to lift the siege.

A Parent's Toolbox

1. *An Intellectual Microscope for Looking at the World of Children.* How do we look at the developing child? First, we should understand how the field of human ecology can bring us inside a child's experiences and see how they are shaped by forces both within and beyond the child, both inside and outside her family. Ecology is the study of relationships between plants and animals on the one hand, and environments (habitats) on the other. Ecologists explore and document how the individual and the habitat influence each other. Like the biologist who learns about an animal by studying its habitat, sources of food, predators, and social practices, the student of human ecology must address how people live and grow in their social environment. And the human ecologist must remember always that human beings live in and through what is in their heads.

Their mental understanding of the world guides their behavior and defines human meaning. *In today's world, every parent must be a human ecologist.*

Remember: when the question is "Does X cause Y?" the best answer is "It depends." This is what guides the human ecologist, the study of the child's development in the specific habitat in which the child lives. It includes family, friends, neighborhood, church and school, as well as less immediate forces that constitute the social geography and cultural climate (for example, laws, institutions, and values) and the physical environment as well.

The exact mix of settings in which the child participates differs from culture to culture and society to society. For example, in some societies, such as ours, formal secondary education is a nearly universal experience for kids (more than 90 percent attend), whereas in others it is rare for youth to attend school beyond the elementary level. The most important characteristic of this ecological perspective is that it both reinforces our inclination to look inside the individual child or parent *and* encourages us to look beyond the individual to the environment for questions and explanations about individual behavior and development.

The key to this approach is the focus on development in context. We cannot predict reliably the future effect of our behavior as parents without knowing something about the rest of the world in which we and our children live. And even then it may be very difficult. For example, much has been made of the decisive role of the early years in a child's later development. National media campaigns urge parents to invest in the first three years as a strategy for ensuring good development later. While there is much truth to this idea, it is too simple to capture the realities of human development.

Do the first three years matter a great deal? Yes. Are the first three years destiny? Does early deprivation predict later dysfunction? After reviewing all the evidence in his book *The Myth of the First Three Years,* John Bruer concludes with a resounding "It depends." It depends on how dramatically bad the early experience is and what developmental opportunities the child encounters. Later nurturance can overcome many effects of early deprivation unless that deprivation is catastrophic.

We see this in all aspects of child development. The quality of the community in which children are growing up plays a big role in their intellectual development as well as their social behavior. Thus, for example, when psychologist Urie Bronfenbrenner studied genetically identical twins who were separated at birth but grew up in similar communities, he found that they turn out to be much alike, whereas identical twins growing up in dissimilar communities are not nearly so much alike. And according to the research by psychologists Rolf Loeber and David Farrington, whereas in some neighborhoods 60 percent of 10-year-olds who are so plagued by violent bad behavior that they are diagnosed with "conduct disorder" will become seriously violent delinquents, the figure is only 20 percent in other neighborhoods. Recall what we said earlier about Bohman's study, namely that the odds of a child with a biological heritage of criminality becoming a criminal are more than three times greater if the child is growing up in a high-risk family than if he is in a well-functioning family.

As individuals develop, they play an ever more active role in an ever-widening world. Newborns shape the feeding behavior of their mothers but are confined largely to cribs or laps, and have limited means of communicating their needs and wants. Ten-year-olds, on the other hand, influence numerous adults and other children in many different settings and have many ways of communicating. The adolescent's world is still larger and more diverse, as is the teen's ability to influence that world. Individuals and environments negotiate and renegotiate their relationships, each influencing and changing the other. Neither is constant; each depends on the other.

An ecological approach helps us discover the connections among seemingly unrelated events. It also can help us see that what often seems like an obvious solution may only make the problem worse. The First Law of Ecology is that "you can never do just one thing." Every parent needs to understand this. It means that we as parents must always be sensitive to the fact that our actions may have unintended consequences.

2. *A Periscope for Seeing the World Through the Eyes of Each Child's Individual Temperament.* Children come into the world with different dispositions. Some are active; some are passive. Some are sensitive; some are insensitive. Some are rhythmic; some chaotic. If you don't have children, it is easy to disbelieve in temperament. "All children are the same," you might say. If you have only one child, it's still possible to disbelieve in temperament. "All children are like my child," you think. But if you have two or more children, you probably believe in temperament. They come in different flavors and varieties.

To be successful with children we must be able to see the world through their eyes. While experience plays a big role in how children see the world (as we will see later), temperament does as well. Indeed, temperament filters every experience a young child has—for example, whether he or she finds novelty exciting or frightening, whether the child is a pleasure to be around or a pain in the neck.

The periscope is vital to parenting success. It enables us to see the world as our child experiences it, and showing the child how to make sense of the world in a way that leads to successfully coping with it is vital to parenting success. According to the classic research conducted by Alexander Thomas and Stella Chess, most children can be classified as "easy," "difficult," or "slow to warm up," based on their initial patterns of activity, responsiveness, ease of soothing, and robustness. More-recent research refines these categories further. For example, psychiatrist Stanley Greenspan identifies five types of difficult children that we will consider in Chapter 6. But the fact remains that temperament is a factor in the developmental equation, and understanding it is empowering for both parents and children.

Parents need to ponder their child's temperament. Being a good observer of temperament early on can help parents plan their strategies more effectively and be more aware of the special and individual nature of their child. Children are not like identical cookies cut from the same cutter. They are more like different pastries: some are cookies, some are donuts, some are apple turnovers.

3. *A Spiritual Fulcrum for Moving the Child to a Positive Place.* The ancient Greek scientist-philosopher Archimedes, who invented the fulcrum, said, "Give me somewhere to stand and I will move the earth." When it comes to moving the world of the family, the ultimate fulcrum is spirituality. There is no more powerful influence on human development; nothing else is so sustaining in difficult times. The good news is that most adults recognize this fact. A survey conducted by the Gannett News Service revealed that 84 percent of Americans think spiritual or religious belief is essential to a happy life. This awareness of the central importance of spirituality is a good starting point for parenting.

Human beings are not just animals with complicated brains. We understand ourselves best when we see ourselves as spiritual beings having a physical experience. This includes being aware that your spiritual existence is the primary fact of your life, recognizing yourself as a spiritual being first and foremost. Even for people who see themselves as religious, this recognition often requires a basic shift: from a focus on the material self first and consciousness second, to the spirit first and the body second.

What do we need to make this shift? One requirement is organizing your life around a spiritual reality. What does that mean? It means living your life with the sense of knowing a

Higher Power, a spiritual source, a Creator, or a benevolent higher spiritual being. Some people don't recognize a single Higher Power, but they do acknowledge a common connection to all life. A second requirement is believing yourself to be connected in spirit to the larger reality. This leads to an appreciation for our relationship to other people as spiritual beings. And a third is an appreciation that soul-searching is one important way to discover truth about human experience.

Soul-searching can expand our basic stories of the physical ("I am born; I live; I die.") by connecting them to the eternal realities of spirituality. Recognizing the spiritual realm is vital for making the most of the other aids in the parent's toolbox; spiritual parenting is the core of being an observant and mindful parent, and thus the key to relieving the siege on parents.

4. *A Developmental Calculator for Tallying Up the Accumulation of Risks and Opportunities in a Child's Life.* The presence or absence of any single risk or opportunity rarely tells the story about a person's development. Human beings can handle challenges and difficulties so long as their number does not overwhelm us by exceeding the protective opportunities available to us. Risks, such as neurological damage or chronic child abuse, increase the odds of experiencing harm. Opportunities are the resources and assets we bring to bear in coping with the risks—for example, a strong sense of optimism or having at least one person who is unambiguously and positively attached to you. These include internal resources (like an easy versus a difficult temperament) and external assets (like a loving grandparent versus a rejecting parent). What predicts harm to a child's development is the buildup of harmful factors combined with a lack of resources to compensate. Children are resilient, but they do have their limits. Children suffer when the number of strikes against them increases to three or four, or more—for example, poverty, mental illness, child abuse, and exposure to racism—particularly when these hazards accumulate without a

compensatory buildup of favorable factors. Once overwhelmed, children are likely to be highly sensitive to whatever additional negative influences they encounter.

It's a juggling act. If we give you one tennis ball, you can toss it up and down with ease. Give you two, and you can still manage easily. Add a third, and it takes special skill to juggle them, but you can learn to manage. Make it four, and you will drop them all. Four is too many unless you have a teacher who shows you how to learn more advanced juggling. So it is with risks.

The liberating message of this approach is that life need not be risk-free for our children to develop successfully, that if we can inject compensatory opportunities into our children's lives we can expect to see positive results—so long as we can prevent their coping capacity from being overwhelmed. If there are one or two risks beyond our immediate control, they need not be destructive.

At the same time, a buildup of risks should be an urgent warning, telling us to protect our children and to marshal our resources to build opportunity factors for them. For example, when parents ask, "Can my child cope with divorce?" we respond, "It depends." It depends on what else is in their developmental equation, how many other risks there are in the child's life, and how many opportunities are available to compensate.

One area in child development research that illustrates risk accumulation is the study of intellectual development. As risks like poverty, parental incapacitation, mistreatment, and large family size accumulate, intellectual development suffers, and children are less likely to have the cognitive strength to master the challenges they face. In a study by psychologist Arnold Sameroff and his colleagues, 11-year-olds with two or fewer risks had above-average IQ scores (113), while those with four or more had below average IQ (93). Average or above intellectual competence is important because it is in itself an opportunity in dealing with life. When risks accumulate, youths achieve less. Then, as a result of lowered achievement, they devalue themselves. With self-devaluation, youths come to lack the reservoir of self-esteem they need to deal with negative peer influences in their communities. It always comes back to the combination of risk and opportunity when figuring out a child's developmental equation. The calculator for totaling up risks and opportunities is an essential tool for making sense of the lives children lead.

5. *The Glue Stick of Resilience for Holding Together a Child's World in Difficult Times.* Human beings are adaptive and resourceful, but resilience is not unlimited, automatic, or universal. Under numerous serious threats in unsupportive environments, no child may escape unscathed, no matter how well-equipped he or she may be temperamentally. Every child has limits. Much is made in the scientific literature and the popular press of resilience. Although defined in numerous ways, resilience generally refers to an individual's ability to bounce back from adverse experiences, to avoid long-term negative effects, or otherwise to overcome developmental threats. Every one of us knows someone whose life is a testament to resilience. The concept of resilience rests on a key research finding: Although any specific negative influence increases the odds of a particular negative outcome, most children escape severe harm.

However, as the concept of resilience has been promoted in ever-wider circles, there is concern that it can easily be misused or misunderstood. Three limitations are especially important for a parent's conceptual toolbox. First, resilience is not absolute; virtually every youth has a breaking point. Research conducted by psychiatrist Bruce Perry on the impact of trauma and deprivation on brain development leads him to assert that kids are "malleable" rather than "resilient," in the sense that each threat costs them something. What is more, as psychologist Patrick Tolan points out, in some environments virtually all youths demonstrate the negative effects of highly stressful and threatening environments. In his Chicago data, for example, *none* of the minority adolescent males in environments of highly dangerous and threatening low-income neighborhoods outside the family *combined with* low-resource/high-stress families was resilient at age 15. Resilience was measured by the adolescent's continuing for a two-year period *neither* to be more than one grade level behind in school *nor* to require professional mental health services for psychological problems.

Second, resilience in gross terms may obscure real costs to the quality of an individual's inner life. Some people manage to avoid succumbing to the risk of *social* failure as defined by poverty and criminality but nonetheless experience real harm in the form of diminished capacity for successful intimate relationships. Thus, even apparent social success—performing well in the job market, avoiding criminal activity, and creating a family—may obscure some of the costs to individuals of being resilient. Their inner lives may be fraught with emotional damage—to self-esteem and intimacy, for example. Though resilient in social terms, they may be severely wounded souls. This has long been evident in comparing the resilience of boys versus girls. Boys who succumb to the accumulation of risks have long been prone to act-out in explicitly antisocial behavior (juvenile delinquency), while girls have been more likely to respond with self-destructive behavior and internalized symptoms, such as stomachaches, nightmares, and wretchedly low self-esteem. Does this mean that girls are more resilient than boys? A simple accounting of social success variables might lead us to think so. However, if we take into account the full range of harm, we can see that such an answer would be wrong. Kids adapt—for better and for worse.

Third, resilience does not mean moral superiority. The youth who demonstrates resilience has extraordinary attributes and resources that the nonresilient child does not have. Being unable to protect oneself against the accumulation of risk factors does not constitute moral turpitude. Some environments are too much for anyone, and to use the concept of resilience as a basis for moral judgment in these settings may be inappropriate and unfair. We have seen this firsthand when testifying as expert witnesses in youth homicide trials. In one case, while seeking to discredit our expert testimony on the role of trauma in shaping youthful behavior, the prosecutor used the concept of resilience in precisely this manner. In his cross-examination, he asked why the defendant was not as resilient as other kids. His exact words were, "What's wrong with this boy that he is not resilient?" That's not fair and it's not good science; it leads to judging and blaming in ways that are unethical and bad science.

6. *A Psychological Tape Measure for Mapping a Child's World.* One of the most important aspects of children's development is the social maps they draw of the world. Each map is both the product of past experience and the cause of future experience. Some children see themselves as powerful, secure countries, surrounded by allies. Others see themselves as poor little islands, surrounded by an empty ocean or hostile enemies.

Such representations of the world reflect a child's intellectual ability—the cognitive competence of knowing the world in an objective sense—but they also indicate moral and emotional inclinations. Children develop social maps, and then they live by them.

In early childhood, the outlines of these social maps begin to emerge. What we commonly call *attachment* is the first such map. It reflects the way an infant understands the social environment. Some infants have a strong, positive map of attachment and live a life of responsiveness and security. For them, it provides a foundation for exploration—physically and emotionally—because it provides a secure base of human operations, a secure homeland. Without this starting point in attachment, the individual is psychologically homeless, and the social map begins to emerge without appropriate boundaries, allies, and orientation to emotional north, south, east, and west. Cultures differ in the precise components of these early social maps. For example, in some societies fathers provide intimate care for infants and emerge in their attachment maps early on, whereas in other societies fathers do not emerge in childhood social maps until later in life. But the universal truth is that someone must be "on the map."

The famous psychoanalyst of childhood Erik Erikson proposed that children must find their way through a series of major challenges en route to a healthy adulthood. These "crises" require that the child construct a social map that will show the way. The first potential roadblock is "basic trust vs. distrust." Does the child come to know the world as a reliable place, where needs are met (basic trust), or as a chaotic place where needs go unmet (basic distrust). If children can navigate through this challenge, they continue down the road of development. Other potential roadblocks lie ahead, such as becoming competent in dealing with bodily issues like toilet training, developing a balanced approach to adult authority, and establishing a positive identity.

The social map continues to develop in ways that reflect the child's experience and emerging capacities. What is more, the social map more and more becomes the *cause* of experience. By adolescence, a youth is acting constantly upon the basis of the information within the map. The youth whose map contains allies acts confidently and securely, and increasingly finds the positive places in life. The youth whose map renders him or her as an insignificant speck, stuck off in a corner, accrues more and more negative experiences. An abused teenager put it this way: "When I meet somebody new, right away I do something bad, so I know where I stand with them."

We worry about the conclusions about the world contained in a youth's social map. Will it be "Adults are to be trusted because they know what they are doing," "People will generally treat you well and meet your needs," "I am a valued member of my society," and "The future looks bright to me"? Or will it be "Strangers are dangerous," "School is a dangerous place," "I feel all alone," and "All I see in my future is more disappointment and failure"?

7. *A Social Geiger Counter for Isolating Cultural Poisons in the Child's Experience.* The social environment can poison the development of children and youth much as the physical environment can undermine their physical well-being. This is especially true for kids who are especially vulnerable to developmental harm because of a difficult temperament or emotional disability. Parents need a social Geiger counter to detect and measure these poisons, particularly if they are raising a temperamentally vulnerable child.

The term *social toxicity* parallels the concept of physical toxicity as a threat to human well-being and survival. A socially toxic environment contains widespread threats to the development of identity, competence, moral reasoning, trust, hope, and the other features of social maps that make for success in school, family, work, and the community.

What are the social and cultural poisons that are psychologically equivalent to lead and smoke in the air, PCBs in the water, and pesticides in the food chain? Feelings of fear about the world, rejection by adults outside the family, violent trauma, absence of adult supervision and inadequate exposure to positive adult role models, economic insecurity, a shallow materialist culture, and weak relationships with the neighborhood and the larger community.

Just as some children are more vulnerable than others to poisons in the ground and in the air, some are more vulnerable to factors like poor role models. Emotionally troubled and temperamentally vulnerable children are like psychological asthmatics. Young children are most vulnerable to aspects of life that threaten the availability and quality of care by parents and other caregivers, while adolescents are most vulnerable to toxic influences in the broader culture and community.

Adolescence is the crystallization of childhood experience, so the youths most at risk are those who develop psychological disabilities in childhood and then face social deprivation and trauma in adolescence. Like social weather vanes, they can indicate the direction of social change in their societies. Which cultural and social pathologies are strongest in a society will generally be most evident in the lives of these youths. It can be drugs in Eastern Europe, prostitution in Thailand and the Philippines, or murderous violence in the United States. We saw this clearly in our work with incarcerated violent youth, as reported in our book *Lost Boys*. Those boys were made vulnerable by temperament and family dysfunction, which they spit back at society in the form of violent delinquency. Trauma is the most obvious and directly damaging form of social toxicity.

Trauma involves psychological as well as philosophical wounds. Both affect the prospects for child development. Trauma can arise from coming face to face with extreme danger and uncontrollable feelings of terror at the same time. *Posttraumatic stress disorder* (PTSD) is the term mental health professionals give to this state. Its components typically include reexperiencing the trauma (through recurrent dreams and flashbacks), numbing of responsiveness in day-to-day life, emotional detachment from others, and a pattern of distorted feelings related to the traumatic experience, such as guilt about having survived while others did not.

What is only beginning to become clear is what happens to youth when the dangers they face are not discrete events but rather become the fabric of life. This is the difference between *acute* danger (for example, when a deranged individual enters a normally safe school and opens fire with a rifle) and *chronic* danger (as when ongoing gang warfare makes streets and schools a battleground in which even innocent bystanders are in jeopardy).

Future orientation is important for youth as a motivation to learn the rules and roles of adult society. Trauma undermines future orientation. Observers who have identified a pattern of extreme threat to future orientation call it *terminal thinking.* Terminal thinking is most clearly evident when, in response to the question, "What do you expect to be when you are 30 years old?" a youth answers, "Dead." This outcome is most likely when danger comes from social conditions that overwhelm day-to-day social reality, as can happen during war or when a youth's neighborhood is taken over by chronic violent crime.

The therapy of choice in situations of chronic danger is the creation of a new positive reality for the youth, one that can stand up to the natural conclusions a severely traumatized youth is likely to draw otherwise: "I'm weak and worthless," "You can't rely upon adults," and "The only way to be safe is to escape or to get them before they get you." When support is at hand and the youth can see the meaning and value of the social options available, he may respond positively, but it will not happen automatically. Every American youth may be affected when the mass media reinforces the view that the world around kids is uncontrollably dangerous and that there is little we can do about it. As parents we know that there is danger in the world, but that the more we wallow in that danger, the more we reduce our chances for replacing it with a sense of security and meaningfulness.

8. *The Moral Compass of Character.* Some people like to think morality is simple: right or wrong, say yes or say no. But in fact, the modern world is a confusing place when it comes to morality and values. The mass media bombards kids with diverging messages about sex, violence, truth, and loyalty. Chil-

dren and youth often have less-than-perfect parents—for example, those who preach the importance of keeping one's word and then get divorced.

The moral compass of character is the tool parents need to help steer children and youth through the ethical complexities of the lives we actually live as opposed to life in storybook fiction. Character education is about the core values that we will *strive* to live by, the standards we will set for ourselves as decent people, knowing full well we don't always measure up. Character takes us away from absolute do's and don'ts and toward evaluating our imperfect attempts to be good in light of how well our behavior conforms to the core values of trustworthiness, respect, responsibility, fairness, caring, and citizenship. The real test for a parent is to answer this question: "If you had the choice of giving your child a million dollars or a solid character, which would you choose?" not "Are you a morally perfect person?" We are not perfect, but we can seek to live with character.

Just as schools can use character as a moral compass in developing and evaluating their programs, activities, and philosophy of education, so can parents while making decisions about family life and child rearing. Amid all the confusion and the temptations and the blind alleys of modern life, we can always gain clarity by asking, Does this contribute to the character development of my child? If it doesn't, we must go back to the drawing board to find a new strategy and alternative child-rearing tactics.

9. *A Psychological Jack for Supporting Children as They Build Character and Competence.* Human beings are social beings. We are more than individuals. This is why social support is so important to us. Relationships nurture us and give us information about our behavior, about how well we are living up to our values. Adequate social support enhances a child's development. It does so directly, by exposing the child to non-

parental adults who care about the child and the child's character. And it does so indirectly, by assisting parents to do right by children.

In contrast to a socially impoverished environment—in which children and parents lack enduring supportive relationships and protective behaviors—in a socially supportive environment, families are part of a network of relationships that provide guidance and emotional validation. Parents need the care and love of their community just as much as children do.

The socially rich environment includes people who are not drained of the energy it takes to care for others. Such individuals can afford to give to and share with others, because the balance of needs and resources in their own personal lives markedly favors the latter. These are the neighbors and friends who provide protective behaviors for kids. They help parents keep children safe, everything from keeping an eye on them, to offering assistance day-to-day or with emergencies, or even intervening on a child's behalf (to reporting maltreatment to protective service agencies). These individuals become one aspect of the socially rich neighborhood.

In contrast, socially impoverished neighborhoods lack such people and operate on a scarcity economy when it comes to social relations. Fear of exploitation, of being a burden or excessively beholden, suppresses mutuality. For example, residents may avoid neighboring acts because they can open a Pandora's box of requests—a negative prospect if one distrusts the caregiving practices of one's neighbors.

Social impoverishment is not synonymous with economic poverty. Not all poor neighborhoods are socially impoverished, and many affluent neighborhoods are. A financially affluent social environment may lack the kind of enduring support systems that families need to provide positive role models, caring adult supervision, and a sense of personal validation.

10. *A Set of Multicultural Keys for Unlocking Cultural Re-*

sources to Meet a Child's Social Challenges. Parenting is a cultural enterprise, grounded in values, beliefs, and assumptions about right and wrong, and about how children develop. For example, most Japanese and Tibetan parents believe that babies should sleep in the same bed with their mother for the first three years of life, whereas most American parents believe they should sleep alone in their cribs as soon as possible. But cultural differences are not fixed and absolute, and parents are not limited to their own culture for ideas about child rearing. Multiculturalism rests on the belief that each culture has something to teach, and something to learn, from every other culture, and using these keys can unlock social resources.

It should come as no surprise that cultures differ. Each is one people's solutions to the general issues of life. This implies that no culture has all the answers for all situations. As conditions change—particularly when that change is rapid—a culture's traditional solutions may become obsolete. This is one point at which parents may turn to other cultures for advice on how to apply basic values to novel situations that they may face in raising children.

Similarly, cultures that have changed in response to new social conditions may make mistakes, and once having done so may lose touch with their earlier values and beliefs. Cultural change may mean wrong turns and dead ends, as well as pathways to improved human development. In such cases a culture may need access to traditional models to reclaim its own heritage. Sometimes, modern societies can teach traditional societies how to deal with modernization. In other cases, traditional cultures can teach modern ones how to respond more effectively to enduring human needs that have become obscured or masked by modern life. For example, more and more American parents are looking to traditional cultures for advice about sleeping arrangements for babies, and the co-sleeping approach is gaining favor as a way to enhance connection and feelings of security.

Multiculturalism is essential because all cultures have evolved in response to basic human dilemmas—*situations to which no response is 100 percent satisfactory.* There is always a human dilemma in balancing the needs of the group with those of the individual, the needs of the individual with those of the family, women's needs with men's, and the needs of adults with those of children.

Conclusion

When asked how he went about his work, the great artist Michelangelo responded in a way that we can make use of in understanding contemporary parenting issues. He said that if given a block of stone and asked to carve an angel, he simply took his hammer and his chisel and carved away anything that did *not* look like an angel. We must adopt a similar approach. Armed with a vision of the good life, from our philosophical, religious, and ideological roots we must take up the tools from our conceptual toolbox and carve away all that is inconsistent with our vision of what we want for our offspring and for ourselves.

Parents are not powerless. Our goal is to equip parents to understand their situation better, as the starting point for effective action. The individualistic and judgmental nature of American culture does us all a disservice, with its emphasis on action, blame, and vindication. We were speaking to an assembly of school administrators a couple of months after the Columbine High School shooting and had reached the point when the floor was open for questions. A middle-aged man in the front row raised his hand to make this statement: "I can guarantee that my boy would never do something like those boys did. It *must* be the parents' fault."

We are tempted to envy his self-confidence, but we don't share it. Successful parents who validate themselves on the basis of how well their kids are doing tempt fate; their arrogance invites disaster. Are they really totally different from parents whose kids have serious problems? Many of these parents are as sure that they are the cause of their child's downfall as another parent is that he is the reason for his child's successes. Our parental toolbox teaches us that neither of these parents may be correct. Both are underestimating the importance of children's temperaments and the social environments around them.

All parents need to delve into the parental toolbox and take another look at parenting, with open eyes and hearts, with a humility born of an understanding grounded in developmental science, and which is more insightful than "business as usual" in American culture. Each of us needs to learn Lesson 1 for parenting in the twenty-first century, the lessons contained in our conceptual toolbox. Each of us should heed the ancient maxim, "There but for the grace of God go I."

Lesson: To regain control, you must first see clearly the forces around and inside your family, and to do so you must reach into the parental toolbox and use those tools to understand more deeply than ever before.

3

Dealing with an "Impossible" Child

Difficult Children Are Born:
Impossible Children Are Made

What do you think we mean when we speak of an "impossible" child? For some of you that is a theoretical question, since your children are well behaved, easy to manage, and without behavior problems. Or you may have two or more children, with only one causing problems for the entire family. But even if all your children are easy to raise, perhaps you know a child who is a trying and exhausting challenge. Perhaps this child is a niece or a nephew, a neighbor's or a friend's or coworker's child. Some parents we have interviewed say these are *the children who try parents' souls.*

When we use the word "impossible," we mean a child who is out of control, who is self-destructive or antisocial, or both. We mean a child who pushes parents to their limits and beyond, who exasperates them despite their best efforts to find constructive and effective solutions. Some children are actively engaged in obnoxious and aggressive behaviors. They are the little dictators who order their parents around and regularly throw temper tantrums when they don't get what they want. Or they are aggressive with other children, and parents are constantly responding to complaints from other children and adults. "He hit me!" "She hurt me!" "Your child took my child's toy." "My child is afraid of your child." And so on. Other types of difficult children are passively whiny and unpleasant. They drag their parents down with their constant complaining and dissatisfaction. Some are depressed. Whatever the behavior, many have problems and act in ways that are never quite understood by parents or mental health professionals. There's a question mark hanging regarding what could be the cause of the child's intolerable or mystifying behavior.

This can leave parents feeling demoralized and helpless. Our goal in this chapter is to begin to use our parenting tools to understand difficult children, and to offer some ideas about why parents face these challenges.

In his book *The Explosive Child*, psychologist Ross Greene provides numerous profiles of "impossible" children, and the effects they have on their parents and siblings. One parent reports, "People who don't have a child like Jennifer don't have a clue about what it's like to live like this. Believe me, this is not what I envisioned when I dreamed of having children. This is a nightmare." A mother of our acquaintance says, "It's humiliating. I feel like such a failure. Every day I wake up hoping it will be better, and some days are okay. But then something will set Robert off again."

After the publication of *Lost Boys*, we heard from many parents with impossible children. Here's what one parent wrote via e-mail:

My son's behavior problems were first noted and therapy sought at age 3 in preschool. I could write a book about all of the things that have been tried over the past eight years to help him change his behavior. I could make a psychiatrist's head spin just by reeling off all of the medication trials we have done. And I could drive myself crazy trying to find an answer. I have a master's degree in clinical psychology, and I look at my son and feel like a sixth-grade dropout. My husband and I do not promote violence, do not buy violent video computer games. We are active participants in our children's lives, and we are stuck. His aggression, violent outbursts, lack of attachment, and subsequent lack of remorse for his negative behavior disturb us greatly. Even worse is his desire for retaliation; the smallest slight is met with lethal petulance. He scares me. Last year he threatened to kill me; this past fall he stole some guns and kept them in his tree house. I find it hard to sleep at night, as does my husband. I have no doubt that my son is deeply sad, that his sadness is agonizing, and his sense of self so small. But his behavior worsens as he gets older. I'm terrified of his adolescence and puberty.

Some parents confront young children who seem destined to be extremely difficult, and who soon become impossible despite the informed actions of parents. But in other cases, we see the role of unwise parenting in creating an impossible child. We remember a cartoon from twenty years ago. In the first panel, two women are at a table in a restaurant. With them is a little boy who is obviously the son of one of the women. Eventually their food arrives. "I want your lunch!" says the little boy, "I want your lunch!" "No," says his mother, "eat your own lunch." "I want your lunch! I want your lunch! I want your lunch," the boy shouts. "Oh, alright," his mother says finally, handing him her lunch. "Here. Have my lunch, but be quiet."

Some time passes. Now the boy begins to take off his pants in the restaurant. "Stop that!" his mother says. "You can't take off your pants in the restaurant." "Take off my pants! Take off my pants! Take off my pants!" the boy shouts. "Oh, alright," says the mother. "Take off your pants, but be quiet." Soon the boy begins to chant, "You take off your pants, Mommy!" She replies indignantly, "I'm not going to take off my pants here!" "Take off your pants! Take off your pants! Take off your pants!" the boy shouts.

In the final frame of the cartoon, the mother is taking off her pants, as she says to her friend, "He's just impossible if I don't give in to him." The expression of the other woman at the table suggests that it is clear to her that the reason he is impossible is precisely because the mother does give in to him. He was born difficult but was made impossible.

But Ross Greene, and others who know such children well, understand that it is not simply a matter of inept parents. Some children are extremely difficult. They provoke "crazy" behavior from parents. They frustrate strategies that work for other people's children. We sometimes baby-sit for a 12-month-old little girl in our neighborhood. Some of her behavior is difficult to understand, at least at first. For example, in a restaurant she will sometimes begin to stare at a nearby table. She becomes fixated on an adult at that table and can't seem to look away. Eventually, she bursts into a high-pitched scream and begins to cry uncontrollably. Our efforts to soothe her are futile.

As Greene points out, some children are impossible in an explosive way because they just can't manage the world as they experience it. His premise is that "these children do not choose to be explosive and noncompliant—any more than a child would choose to have a reading disability—but are delayed in the process of developing the skills that are critical to being flexible and tolerating frustration or have great difficulty applying these skills when they most need to." Of course, some parents do a better job than others in helping their children develop critical skills for getting along. As we shall see later, most parents *can* do better with these children than most parents typically do. That's the whole point of Greene's book, of course: to help parents do better with these difficult children, to transform them from being impossible to being manageable.

Without such early intervention, these children are headed toward a number of serious problems, patterns of behavior that often become more and more severe, and affect more and more aspects of daily life. Depending upon the turn these problems take, they may end up with a cluster of problems centering around refusing to listen to parents and teachers ("Oppositional Defiant Disorder"). Or they may exhibit extreme difficulty in paying attention to schoolwork ("Attention Deficit/Hyperactivity Disorder"). Some will turn to a chronic pattern of aggression, bad behavior, acting-out, and violating the rights of others ("Conduct Disorder"). In the extreme, they may end up filled with rage and nastiness, ungoverned by moral principles, such as the children and youth described by psychologist Ken Magid and his colleague Carole McKelvey in their book *High Risk: Children Without a Conscience.* A scary prospect for any parent.

Here's how one mother describes it.

The way my son handles blowups—he lets it all build up inside no matter how much I try to help him talk things out, and when it finally bursts, I'm scared of him. Really. I'm scared of him. He punched a hole in the wall the other day, and I ended up calling the sheriff to come talk to him. I can watch how he acts for a couple of days and tell by his behavior that he's going to have a blowup. Sometimes it is over the simplest things. He started punching holes in the wall while he was still in grade school. I was so afraid that the child welfare agency was going to have a look at him and take him away! And I was not the problem. I was trying to love him, and I was just trying to help him any way that I could. But despite my best efforts, things continued to deteriorate. By the following year, he was hanging out with friends that I thought were very nice and polite around parents, but I knew they were involved in negative things. Dan was caught at school with bags of marjoram and oregano, which he was trying to sell as pot. He denied trying to sell this as pot and was suspended for the rest of the year, and consequently failed that year. It was not just that one incident. It was a buildup of things. By then he was very well known by the principal's office. He was always lashing back. He wasn't going to take the teachers' criticism anymore, and he was talking back to them disrespectfully. He had kids who threatened to beat him, and he got in a big fight one time and actually broke his hand from hitting another youth right in the face. He was well known, and the school was ready to get rid of him. They wanted to really bad. He was now 12 or 13.

Of course, by then I was having trouble coping with all these problems because as a single mother, I never get a break. I'm trying to deal with it the best I can, but the stress becomes unbearable. Eighth grade was disastrous from day one. I would get a call from school every single day with complaints that Dan was doing this or Dan was doing that. Eighth grade was just hell for me, and he was just out of control. Totally out of control. He would scream and yell at me, and threaten me. He was just so unbelievably angry. And of course I had taken him to so many therapists, and he was put on so many different kinds of medication. But nothing ever seemed to help. Then he got to the point where he became severely, severely depressed. And he started talking about death. Out of the blue, he'd say something that was just really out of character, something like "I wonder what would happen if I jumped off a bridge." It was so out of character, and it scared me to death! So I had him hospitalized. They put him on a suicide watch. That was truly one of the hardest things I could have ever done. Of course, Dan would say it was nothing, but parents who hear their kid talk about dying and death for three months can't dismiss it as "Oh, it's nothing." When he got out of the hospital, I had a complete breakdown. And I mean a *complete* breakdown. I couldn't even tie my shoes. That was about one month after Dan got out of the hospital. I couldn't get out of bed, and I couldn't go to work. The stress was just too much. I just couldn't take it anymore. Then I was the one to end up in the hospital! I was put on medication. But when you reach a point where you just can't even move, you can't talk, you can't get out of bed—you have nowhere to go from there but to the hospital. Through trying various medications, they finally got me to a point where I could cope. But I know that a lot of that stress was because Dan was so out of control and I felt that I couldn't do anything to help him and he was going down fast. Nothing I did was slowing down his descent. It was a combination of Dan and his problems with school, and his problems with suicidal feelings, and I had just gotten a new job that was very stressful, and I had bought a new house and was trying to be everything and everybody at all times, trying to build a better life for my son, only to watch him get worse. There was something about him being in the hospital that I couldn't give him: In the hospital, he was safe. And I was scared to death of his being back.

What Happens to Impossible Children?

What does the future hold for impossible children? What do they become in adulthood? Bringing our ecological perspective to bear, we know that the best scientific answer is, "It depends." It depends a great deal on the kind of resources their parents and schools can bring to bear. When parents have the resources to support them, or when the community subsidizes them, these children may end up in residential treatment centers, therapeutic wilderness programs, and specialized boarding schools.

Tragically, some impossible children don't even make it to adulthood. They are more likely to die in accidents, from what public health professionals now call nonintentional injuries. For example, their anger and out-of-control behavior shows up in their driving. Road rage, reckless driving, and drinking are a deadly combination. Such youngsters are also more likely to die in acts of violence (intentional injuries), since they provoke aggression from others.

Children who are not only impossible but also live in emotionally and spiritually deprived environments are likely to end up in detention centers, juvenile prisons, or mental hospitals. The statistics on the kids who develop chronic patterns of conduct disorder are particularly disturbing. Researchers Loeber and Farrington showed that on average, 30 percent of kids with a pattern of chronic aggression, bad behavior, acting-out, and violating the rights of others by age 10 become serious violent delinquents in adolescence (versus 3 percent for other kids). Prisons are full of such individuals—mainly males—who by age 10 were so troubled and troubling that they had been diagnosed with "conduct disorder" and eventually "antisocial personality disorder," and the system had already locked them away. We came to know many such boys while writing *Lost Boys*. A study of New York State's juvenile prisons revealed that 85 percent of the adolescent inmates had been diagnosed with conduct disorder as children. Not surprisingly, most of these kids had vulnerable temperaments and grew up facing the terrible challenges of hostile social environments.

Why Are Some Kids Impossible?

Some kids become impossible because they carry a heavy genetic burden or are damaged at birth or in early infancy. Some of the most devastating forms of mental illness are loaded with genetic influences that provoke severely distorted patterns of thinking and feeling—schizophrenia and depression, for example. Autism, too, is linked to genetic factors, although recent research suggests that a growing number of cases are related to a breakdown in the infant's immune system, most likely because of toxins in the physical environment or an adverse reaction to childhood vaccinations. Profound mental retardation can arise from genetic causes, pregnancy and birth problems, and early traumas that adversely affect brain development. Some kids are severely abused. All these influences can contribute to a child's becoming impossible, even though we know that how children are treated will shape their social and emotional development, regardless of genetic problems, in most cases.

But what about difficult kids growing up in America *before* our society became so toxic? A study by Harvard psychologist Avshalom Caspi and his colleagues tells a disturbing story from pre–World War II history. Caspi's study focused on kids born in 1928, who by age 10 were plagued by severe and frequent temper tantrums. Some 38 percent of the boys and 29 percent of the girls fit this pattern of screaming and thrashing about that is common among 2- and 3-year-olds. Most children overcome this common developmental issue by age 8. But for the kids in the study, temper tantrums had become a way of life. Physical outrage ("biting, kicking, striking, and throwing things") and verbal explosions ("swearing, screaming, and shouting accompanied by marked emotional reactions . . . anger completely dominated behavior") had become the norm, and tantrums occurred anywhere from once a month to several times a day.

The researchers followed these kids for more than half a century, beginning in 1928. What they found is sobering. The general trend for boys and girls was a lifelong pattern of disappointment and social failure. At a time (the 1940s) when high school graduation was becoming the standard for normal development, temper tantrum–ridden boys were less likely to graduate from high school and were thus at a disadvantage occupationally. Middle-class ill-tempered boys had trouble holding onto their middle-class status. At age 40, 53 percent were in jobs that were less prestigious than the jobs their fathers held when they were 40 (compared with 28 percent of the even-tempered boys). When they joined the military (as did 70 percent of all the boys because they came of age during the Korean War), ill-tempered boys achieved lower ranks. The work history of ill-tempered boys was more erratic than that of their even-tempered peers, particularly if they were in low-status jobs, where their oppositional behavior was likely to be precipitated by bosses and supervisors.

The effects extended to family life as well. The ill-tempered boys were half as likely as the even-tempered boys to be in an intact first marriage by age 40. Half were divorced (versus 22 percent of the even-tempered boys). And when rated at age 40 by independent judges, the ill-tempered boys were found to be more undercontrolled, irritable, and moody. Impossible boys tended to become impossible students, workers, husbands, and fathers.

What about the girls? Because they grew up at a time when it was rare for women to have careers, few of the effects of being an ill-tempered girl showed up directly in occupational successes and failures. Where the effects did show up was in their marriages. At age 40, 40 percent of the ill-tempered girls were married to men whose occupational status was lower than that of the girls' fathers at that age. Ill-tempered girls were more likely to be divorced: 26 percent versus 12 percent. They had more marital conflicts and were more dissatisfied with their marriages. Finally, their husbands and children rated them as "less adequate and more ill-tempered mothers."

Impossible children can have lifelong social and emotional disabilities. The path is not fixed, however. Some ill-tempered children triumphed over their emotional bad habits and difficult temperaments. But how do kids get to be temper tantrum–ridden and otherwise impossible in the first place? We find the answer, as always, in the combination of a child's vulnerable temperament and a family's mode of operation.

Angry Early

Childhood anger springs from many sources. Our ecological understanding leads us to look at social, cultural, psychological, and biological influences. And the role of temperament in setting the stage is very important. Psychologist Lewis Lipsitt speaks compellingly about the foundations of anger in the infant.

> I believe that anger is present in babies, even newborns. . . . They make tight fists, their muscles tense, and they pull their legs up to their chest. . . . Many lifelong patterns of angry behavior are acquired in the context of early experience. It is extremely important how the child is responded to when angry. These settings teach the child lifelong patterns either of adaptive or maladaptive ways of handling anger-provoking events.

When the child learns successful strategies based upon communication and socially acceptable behavior, anger takes its normal place in the array of human emotions. When the child learns antisocial strategies, anger can become the dominant theme.

The classic research of psychologist Gerald Patterson charts one unfortunate course that leads to impossibility. Patterson and his colleagues found that some families develop poor habits of interaction, which often start with parents misunderstanding and losing track of cause and effect with their children. For example, a parent may believe that giving in to a crying child "works" because the child stops crying, but fails to see the long-term consequences of this giving in when it extends beyond early infancy.

Decades of research by British psychiatrist John Bowlby shows us that being highly responsive to infants in *the first six months* of life does work to give the child a sense of security and trust: "The world meets my needs; I can trust the world." And the cared-for child becomes more responsive to adult requests. Bowlby believed that giving in was advantageous to an infant's development through the first year. But beyond that, it begins to have the opposite effect.

As children move into the second and third years of their lives and beyond, they have two kinds of temper tantrums. The first reflects a child being overwhelmed by unmet needs and breaking down. The second is an ever more deliberate tactic on the child's part to control the parent. What parents sometimes don't realize is that when they can't differentiate between the two and give in to the second, "instrumental" type of tantrum, the child is learning the lesson "I can get what I want by complaining long and loud enough." These are the temper tantrum–ridden children studied by Caspi.

Patterson learned many things about effective interaction between parents and young children. He learned that well-functioning relationships have a high ratio of positive responses versus negative exchanges. In effect, parents put a lot of emotional money in the bank so they can draw upon that reserve to deal with negative behavior when it arises. But knowing how to deal effectively with negative behavior is the key to preventing a child from becoming impossible. In particular, Patterson noted that the biggest challenge for parents is handling punishment effectively.

Parents need to be positive toward the child as a general rule, but must also insist that negative demanding behavior fail for the child. It's as the political experts say: "Don't give in to terrorists!" While saying no and sticking to it may be difficult in the short run—a crying, unhappy child at a particular moment when you are already stressed out or preoccupied—establishing authentic authority works in the long run to prevent a pattern of impossibility from arising.

Them Are Us

The cartoon we described earlier in this chapter can teach us a vital lesson: As parents we are not always good observers, either of our own children or our parenting behavior. Gerald Patterson observed this. We can see it too.

The mother in the cartoon seems to be confusing cause and effect. She doesn't see that by giving in to her son, she sustains his obnoxious behavior. Why? Chances are that the immediate relief she experiences from his ceasing to badger her is a powerful reward for the mother—particularly in a public place, where his behavior is highly embarrassing. That, coupled with her emotional bond with the boy, blinds her as an effective observer of their interaction.

We developed the parent's toolbox to help you become fine observers and analysts of your children's behavior (not to mention your own). Understanding how temperament works and why social maps are so important helps you see more clearly why some children are more apt to become impossible. The easily frustrated child (that's one temperament most of us are familiar with) is prone to emotional outbursts. Understanding the subtleties of your child's social maps, you are better equipped to see that your responses are not always comprehended by your child. As the difficult child moves beyond infancy, the "giving" parent may be seen by the child as a "sucker." Harsh words, but somewhat true.

We do not wish to judge and demean parents locked in to unproductive patterns with their children. One of our core principles in understanding parenting is to insist upon empathy, to recognize that "we" are always "they," to force ourselves to remember that "them" are "us." The great Vietnamese Buddhist teacher Thich Nhat Hanh has written in his book *Peace Is Every Step:*

> When you plant lettuce, if it does not grow well, you don't blame the lettuce. You look into the reasons it is not doing well. It may need fertilizer, or more water. You never blame the lettuce. Yet if we have problems with our friends or our family, we blame the other person. But if we know how to take care of them, they will grow well, like lettuce. Blaming has no positive effect at all, nor does trying to persuade using reasons and arguments. That is my experience. No blame, no reasoning, no argument, just understanding. If you understand, and you show that you understand, you can love, and the situation will change.

Of course, many spiritual teachers come to this point naturally. Jesus said, "Judge not lest ye be judged." Connection is the starting point, recognizing that we are all the same. This does not mean we wait passively. We may have to initiate powerful interventions to help the child become better. But we do so on the basis of understanding and love, not blame and punishment.

The Addiction of Impossibility

Listen to Caroline talk about her child-rearing style:

I give in to Robert. I know I do. But he badgers me until I do. As a single parent, I don't have the luxury of having someone on my team. It's always him against me and he is relentless. The relief I get from giving in to him doesn't last long. I realize that. But the peace after his storm is so blessedly wonderful I can't give it up. I guess this is how drug addicts feel. They know they are addicted and they know the more drugs they do, the stronger the addiction will become. But the feeling of relief is so good it's impossible to resist on your own.

This mother is right about the nature of drug addiction, by the way. The delight of being high is motivating, but for the most part, people keep at their habits because they get relief from the negative feelings of doing without the drug. The agony of withdrawal is worth it to them to have temporary relief from feeling lousy most of the time. In psychological terms, this is called negative reinforcement—that is, removal from a negative situation as the reward for acting in a certain way. Relief is hard to resist, even when it is extremely costly and self-destructive. For the addict, it is virtually impossible without a lot of help.

Power struggles often arise inadvertently between parents and young children in the first five years of life, and the consequences may become painfully apparent in early adolescence. Rather than being a time when everything about a child moves in new directions, adolescence is a time of intensification. Although development proceeds throughout the life cycle and continues into old age, adolescence is the time when childhood investments start to pay dividends and childhood patterns start to come to fruition in adolescent behavior and personality.

If childhood problems become deeply ingrained but hidden from parents' understanding, children can reach a point at which they require more therapeutic care than most parents can provide alone. This means professional intervention—as

mild as weekly therapy to as intensive as placement with therapeutic foster parents or in a residential rehabilitation facility.
Patterson's lessons are as valuable as ever: Subtle mistakes in
discipline and limit-setting with temperamentally vulnerable
children in the early years can set the stage for parent-child relations that get caught up in what Patterson calls no-win "coercive cycles" that often require professional assistance to
change. We have seen this firsthand in therapeutic wilderness
programs like Second Nature. Research shows that when such
programs combine physically challenging demands with intensive psychotherapy, they can succeed in retrieving out-of-control kids from patterns of delinquent behavior.

How Bad Is It?

How bad is it? A survey finds that one in five parents believe they have at least one child at home who makes it difficult to live a normal life. Gannett News Service's national
survey (referred to in Chapter 1) found that 82 percent of
adults say children today are less respectful toward their elders than when they were growing up. However, adults of every
generation seem to think contemporary children are less well
behaved than they were in the past. As more than one come-
dian has put it, "Nostalgia just isn't what it used to be." The
ancient Greek philosopher Plato's assessment of "kids today"
is often cited, in which he bemoaned the decline of character
and morality in his society. And recall that it was in the 1950s
that a Broadway musical offered the hit song, "What's the matter with kids today?"

So, are there more impossible kids today than when we were
growing up? One "yes" comes from psychologist Thomas
Achenbach. In 1975 he and his colleagues identified children
who were troubled enough to require professional mental health
intervention. They found that 10 percent of our kids met the
criterion. But when they repeated the study in 1989, they found

that the figure had risen to 18.2 percent—nearly doubling in fifteen years.

It is also clear that more and more children are being identified in schools and homes as being difficult to manage, being defined as hyperactive and unruly. The diagnosis of Attention Deficit/Hyperactivity Disorder (ADHD) has risen in recent decades. We have all seen the reports in the media of elementary-school children—mostly boys—lining up before the school nurse for their afternoon dose of Ritalin.

Autism is increasing as well, as are depression and other psychological problems that make children more difficult to manage and care for. While there is controversy over how much of these increases are due to overzealous and inappropriate diagnoses, the evidence Achenbach and his colleagues have provided persuades us that the increase is real.

Not so long ago, most psychologists and psychiatrists dismissed the idea that teenagers could demonstrate authentic depression. This has changed. In *The Life of a Bipolar Child,* her first-person account of being the parent of a child whose depression eventually led to suicide, Trudy Carlson chronicles both growing awareness of the reality of childhood depression and its increase in American society.

Some people are biologically more vulnerable than others, and the tendency to depression can be inherited by children from their parents. But the fulfillment of this predisposition in a child depends to a large degree on that child's experiences. As the society becomes more poisonous, temperamentally vulnerable children succumb to depression precipitated by fractured relationships, eroding social institutions, collapsing traditions, and our increasingly toxic mass media.

Why?

Why are there more impossible children today? We can put four of our parenting tools to work in answering this question.

Our risk-and-opportunity calculator alerts us to the concentration of causes in the lives of particular children and families. Our understanding of spirituality directs us to look for more than material reasons, into unmet spiritual needs, into a hole in the heart. The psychological tape measure of social maps tells us to measure the subjective reality of how kids come to see the world and their place in it. Our social Geiger counter points us in the direction of detecting cultural and social poisons that undermine positive development. Using these tools, we can point to four principal trends.

First, more seriously premature infants survive today than in the past, and some of these babies face the added complication of having been put at risk because of their mothers' cocaine use or alcohol abuse. Severely premature infants are more challenging to care for than full-term babies. They are born vulnerable, perhaps, but certainly not impossible—very few children are. But they are more prone to physical difficulties, intellectual limitations, and challenging temperaments; they are more likely to become impossible if not handled well. Every newborn needs attentive, loving care. But the pressure is much greater on the parents and community institutions that care for these vulnerable children. All this is compounded when the parents are young and themselves vulnerable because of low income, lack of social support, and unresolved psychological issues.

Second, more and more children are growing up in single-parent families in which one adult is responsible for child rearing, often without the psychological jacks of social support that promote effective parenting. That's a tough assignment for any parent, and it has important ramifications for child rearing. For one thing, single parents are less likely to have a second opinion readily available to them as they deal with the child. For another, a parent alone is more likely to be overwhelmed or worn down by persistent, assertive children. As Caroline, the young mother we quoted earlier, put it: "There was no one else on my team."

The challenges she faced as a single mother are greater in part because she easily can lose perspective on how much she is being controlled and exploited by her child. There isn't another parent at home to validate her sense of violation or, if she unwittingly enables the child's negative behavior, there is no one to help her become more aware of the problem and offer some backup in effectively dealing with it. As a result, lone parents may be willing to tolerate excruciatingly demanding and intense relationships with a child. Were there an intimate supportive partner on the scene, the parent might get a fresh perspective. This is one reason why well-functioning two-parent families have an edge in child rearing.

Ironically, it also may be one reason why stepfamilies have a particularly difficult time, even though the backup is there: The kids who have adapted themselves to a family in which they are used to going one-on-one with a single parent are now "double-teamed." And many resent it. Some struggle mightily against it. Add to that the ambiguity of roles that many stepparents feel, and it is little wonder why difficult children may become impossible when faced with complicated family dynamics that no one fully understands.

Third, the pace and technology of modern life make it ever more likely that children will become impossible. Child rearing takes time—on someone's part. Here's an important proposition: The less time an individual has with a child, the more difficult it is to manage that child, the more assistance it takes to compensate. By the same token, arrangements in a household today may offer parents options to disengage with children that were not so readily available in the past. Consider television.

We will discuss television in more detail in Chapter 9, but here it is worth noting one of the earliest studies of television in the lives of families was done by psychologist Eleanor Maccoby in the early 1950s, when television was first appearing in American households. Among other things, she asked parents how the addition of their first television set had affected parenting.

Most parents told her television made it easier to be a parent. They often said such things as, "It's like putting him to sleep." Maccoby found that interaction patterns in families changed when TV entered the home. Family members spent more time focusing on television and less on each other.

The effect was magnified with the rise of multiple televisions in American households, now the norm. Whereas in the pre-television era a parent had little choice but to interact with a child—and thus invest the time and energy needed to establish authority and discipline—in the television era, parents could create space between themselves and the child. "Go watch TV and leave me alone!" became a viable option, with unknown consequences. Who more than parents of difficult children would be likely to seize upon this option? The likelihood of a difficult child becoming an impossible child increases. And that's not even getting into the matter of what the child is watching on television. Sounds like a vicious cycle, and it is.

Fourth, the time crunch that so many families experience damages child rearing. In today's world, parenting competes with many other demands on our time. Making a living, enjoying our intimate partners, pursuing personal development—all these take time and energy, and time and energy are finite. By definition, child care equals time to care for and supervise children. Good child rearing is not done by remote control. But there is more to it than the minutes and hours spent on the child's development and character. Also at stake is how children interpret the time parents spend with them, and the time they don't. At stake is the nature and quality of their social map, what they learn about who values what, and how they follow through on their values.

Children value their parents' time as much, if not more, than anything else—unless they take it for granted. This may sound like a paradox, but it isn't. Most of us take the really important things in life for granted, so much so that we aren't consciously aware of their importance. What is the most important thing you are doing right now? Here's a hint: It isn't reading this book. You are breathing; your heart is beating. Of course, once we mention those things you can express your appreciation for them.

Could anyone be fully aware in each moment of all the things they usually take for granted? That is the issue that occupies the disciplines of mindfulness, the goal of being fully present in each and every moment of existence. In Buddhism, the effort to achieve this is the central task of human existence (and once it is fully realized, the individual attains the state of enlightenment). To increase our mindfulness requires focus and effort. It requires the fulcrum of spirituality to move us toward appreciation for the present moment.

Who's Taking Time?

What does this have to do with parenting? For one thing, it helps us understand that what children say is most important in their lives is apt to exclude things they take for granted. And it is very difficult to appreciate what you cannot recognize because it is taken for granted. Are our children also hearing the message, "Hurry up and grow up"? One is tempted to conclude that many are, particularly in light of a study conducted by sociologist Howard Bahr and his colleagues. Twenty-five years ago, Bahr's team of investigators repeated questions first posed to teenagers about their parents in the classic Middletown study more than seventy-five years ago. In 1924, 63 percent of the adolescents reported that the most desirable attribute of a father is that he spends time with his children. Only 38 percent placed a premium on mothers who spent time with their children.

Does this mean kids in 1924 didn't value their mothers as much as their fathers? Not really. It means they took their moms for granted. On the other hand, kids appreciated that fathers who spent time with them were doing something special. By 1977, however, things had changed. Sixty-two percent of kids said the most valuable thing about a mother is that she spends time with you (and 68 percent said the same of fathers).

This suggests that maternal involvement has become more valued, but also that children recognize they can't count on their mothers to be available as they once did, any more than they could ever have that expectation of their fathers. Other studies tell us that children are likely to see their fathers as involved if they make a point of doing things that tell the child he or she is present in the father's mind and heart—even if he is not there physically.

But these findings presuppose that someone (typically the mother) is actually there for the child day to day. It is important for both parents to be valued. At the same time, can we find ways to offer children the basic reassurance of commitment that they need? To understand this, we must look at another issue, the pressure on children to replace adult supervision with self-supervision in response to changing roles for mothers and the intransigence of fathers and the larger community.

Are Children Caught Between the Changing Role of Women and the Unchanging Role of Men?

Most women today, even if they are mothers, want to earn a paycheck and be part of the labor force outside the home. They find it conveys a sense of worth and accomplishment. They need the money, financially and psychologically. In 1960, 60 percent of two-parent families could maintain a middle-class lifestyle on one income. Now that figure has dropped below 25 percent. This is an inevitable by-product of our society's increasing focus on money as the definition of human value (and it helps explain why teenagers want to earn money too).

In 1970, 53 percent of the women polled by a *New York Times* survey named "being a mother and raising a family," and 43 percent named "being a homemaker," as one of the two or three "most enjoyable things about being a woman today." The comparable figures for 1983 were 26 percent and 8 percent. "Career, jobs, pay" and "general rights and freedoms" increased from 9 percent to 28 percent and from 14 percent to 32 percent, respectively. In the decades since these findings were released, the issues have become ever more complex and difficult.

Beyond wanting the satisfaction that a paycheck brings, women face basic financial pressures. Families need income-generating mothers, whether it be for affluence (two middle-class workers), protection from low income (two blue-collar workers), or sheer survival (a single parent). Two incomes lift middle-class families into the affluent range and prevent low-income families from slipping into poverty. The demand for getting the most out of parental money-making capacity is leading us to a crisis in child care and supervision, a crisis that most dramatically affects the vulnerable children who are most at risk for becoming impossible.

Who takes care of the children while the parents are out making money? In early childhood, the answer is a relative, a neighbor, or a day care home or center. But during the elementary school years, the pressure grows to move the responsibility for child care onto the shoulders of the child. While some schools provide after-school care—and some parents find neighbors, relatives, or day care centers that will take elementary school children—more and more parents try to cope with the demands of work and the high cost of child care by enlisting children to care for themselves. Necessity is the mother of invention, to be sure, but necessity may also give rise to rationalization.

Is it good for kids to take care of themselves before they enter adolescence? Some children start in self-care at ages 8 or 9. This premature responsibility ends up with kids who are twice as likely to experiment with drugs, alcohol, and sex by the time they are 15. Why?

We all live in a socially toxic environment, that's why. For many children, its negative pressures take their toll unless there are strong forces to counter them. Children need a strong moral compass of character to resist. They need a strong psychological jack in the form of social support to resist. They need a positive social map to resist. If children are to make a go of it in our socially toxic environment, they need *more* rather than less adult supervision, *more* rather than less intensive parenting, to reduce susceptibility to negative peer influences, to negative mass media influences, to the low self-esteem often generated at school. They need *more* rather than less connection with their parents and with other positive adult role models.

And yet the modern economy and parental roles in that economy stimulate and reinforce rationalizations like the following: "Children don't need adults, they need to be free," and "Children can cope with a lot more than we give them credit for," and "Children understand that their parents have to live their own lives too," and "The sooner children grow up, the better off they will be in the long run."

In today's society, parents are likely to believe that young children are capable of assuming early responsibility for self-care and that early demands for maturity are in the child's best interest. They are apt to make decisions based not on what the child needs but what the child can tolerate. Such rationalization leads inevitably to the implication that there is something wrong with children if they cannot meet the demands of adults who are responding to the demands placed on them.

Our world requires more rather than less emotional competence and social skills than ever before. Psychologist Avshalom Caspi and his colleagues put it this way in their study of ill-tempered children: "The need to delay gratification, control impulses, and modulate emotional expression is the earliest and most ubiquitous demand that society places on the developing child, and success at many life tasks depends critically on the individual's mastery of such ego control." That was true of the children they studied who were born in 1928, and it is even more true today because the high demands placed upon children to succeed in school and in the workforce leave little room for impossible children.

Home Alone in a Socially Toxic Environment

Visiting a third-grade classroom in a middle-class suburb, we asked, "How many of you have a grown-up there when you go home after school?" About a third shook their heads and kept their hands down. That's about average for 8-year-olds today; in some places, the figure is higher, even for younger children. By the time kids are 9, a majority are home alone at least some of the time. Some call these kids "latchkey children." Others prefer the term "children in self-care." Whatever you call them, they are at least in part the product of a society that does not greatly value making adequate child care possible for all parents who need it. Many parents—many mothers—have few options. Women need to work in the cash economy. Despite evidence of some shift in traditional role divisions, few men are ready, willing, and able to alter the old patterns that define child care as the mother's responsibility whether or not she works outside the home.

The problem figures most prominently when mothers alone seek to raise their children while dealing with separated or divorced fathers who fail to provide child support payments (and thus force mothers between an economic rock and a hard place). But it lies also with fathers who live with their children but don't assume full responsibility for day-to-day care. It lies with unaccommodating workplace managers and unsympathetic policy-makers.

What child of the 1950s fully appreciated the fact that he or she had two parents? It is doubtful if many did. The only exceptions are where a few children were close to other children who lost their parents to death or separation. Now? Many children sense the precariousness of parental presence and involvement. The good news is, they notice their parents when they are there. The bad news is, many children feel anxious about the durability of family relationships. Conversely, many parents feel guilty that they don't spend enough time with them, guilty that they are not offering a two-parent family, guilty that they are not knowledgeable enough to be "super-parents."

Finally, many parents have come to believe that they owe their children indulgence and the right to run the show. Some may feel they lack the moral credibility to act authoritatively. Some parents may panic that their children won't succeed in the world if they don't give them every possible material and technological advantage, and in so doing miss an essential point. Far more important than any material possession is the moral compass of character, successful strategies for mastering temperamental difficulties, evolving positive social maps, acquiring access to deep, sustaining cultural resources, and having spiritual needs met.

The Difficulty of Seeing What Is in Front of Your Eyes

Impossible children are not merely the product of changing conditions within the home and the community. Some of the difficulty arises from the challenge parents face in understanding their children. Almost all of us are in some profound way blind to our kids as they really are. The German poet Goethe knew this when he wrote: "What is the most difficult of all? That which seems to you the easiest, to see with one's eyes what is lying before them."

Few parents have mastered the concepts and the language we offer in our toolbox. Most of us don't have the ecological perspective at our disposal, so we don't realize the importance of context in shaping cause-effect relationships in child rearing.

Most of us don't understand temperament. Therefore, we think one child-rearing style fits all children. We don't understand the accumulation of risk, so we don't realize that our child may not be able to tolerate a disruption that another child could tolerate simply because our child has already absorbed several risk factors. We don't have the concept of social maps, so we don't realize that the correspondence between objective and subjective reality is always imperfect, and may even be weak. Parents don't have the full range of tools they need. We are surrounded by nails but have no hammer. Or we have only a hammer and are inclined to see every child-rearing issue as a nail. And perhaps, most important, we are not mindful.

A mindful parent is one who can suspend all categories, all preconceptions, and all biases and experience the child directly and without the various distortions that burden normal experience. It is not easy, but it is possible. One father puts it this way:

My son is a very, very difficult child. He is so intense, every little conflict becomes a major confrontation. He is often obstinate, obnoxious and moody, and he is fierce in his power to deny and rationalize everything and shift responsibility for things onto other people. He also has a sweet, delightful side when things are in tune. Thank God for that! When he gets bad grades on his report card, his explanation is always that it's the teacher's fault. When he has a fight with his girlfriend, it is always because she is so difficult and moody. It is tempting to withdraw from him or to attack him verbally as he does me. But I have come to learn that neither strategy works in the long run. Withdrawing only postpones conflict. Fighting back to his verbal salvos only escalates the conflict. What does work is mindfulness. I take the lessons I have learned in meditation and my spiritual practice and apply them to parenting.

What does that mean in practice? The boy's father continues:

It means I cultivate calmness when he is around. I suspend my impulse to judge him or to defend myself. I don't feed his negative emotions. I try to meet his internal uproar with my own peacefulness. I embrace and accept him. It's not easy, and I can't always manage to meet my mindfulness goals. Almost anyone can be calm if he is sitting in a lovely, peaceful retreat center in the mountains. But to achieve such calm when confronted by an out-of-control, obnoxious teenage boy, now that is something! And when I can achieve this calmness I see things so much more clearly, and it works.

The boy gave his father a Father's Day card that read: "Thanks for standing by me." The impossible becomes possible with mindfulness.

Conclusion
It works. Ah, what sweet words for a parent under siege. It works. We will return to the practice of mindfulness in dealing

with temperamentally difficult children in Chapter 6. Are parents doomed to be blind to the realities of how their behavior affects their children's behavior? No.

Lesson: Only by cultivating mindfulness and utilizing the conceptual tools can parents see their children as they are, appreciate how parental behavior contributes to the development of impossible children, and find the road out of impossibility.

4

The Dangerous World Outside Your Front Door

A Child Asks: Am I Safe?

Security is vitally important for a child's well-being. When children feel safe, they relax. When they relax, they start to explore their environment. Parents can see this clearly with babies and toddlers. When a parent or other familiar person is around, a child treats that person as a secure base from which to explore the nearby space. If frightened—perhaps by a loud sound or by the approach of a stranger—the child will quickly retreat to the familiar person.

This is what normal child development looks like. It is so common that it is used by psychologists to assess the quality of children's attachment relations. Children who do not use their parents this way—showing anxiety when separated and relief when reunited—are thought to have a less than adequate attachment relationship. Psychologists describe such children as insecure, ambivalent, avoidant, or disorganized. Thus, for very young children, the question of security is relatively simple. As parents, we remember clearly the physical experience of the clinging, wary child regarding a stranger.

Of course, as children get older, their security needs change. Soon our children are getting on school buses and visiting friends by themselves. Eventually, they go out at night on their own and drive to basketball games and high school dances. But security remains a constant theme for them. Am I safe here? Will I be safe if I go there?

Many children do not feel safe. In some cases, their insecurity is grounded in the physical facts of their day-to-day lives. For some children the danger lies inside their families. Domestic violence is an ugly fact of life for far too many children. Research conducted by sociologists Murray Straus and Barbara Carlson reveals that between 3 million and 10 million children live in families in which there is some physical assault against a parent by a parent or another adult in the home. One in seven children lives in families in which violence is severe—meaning millions of children. Spousal or partner abuse violates a child's sense of trust and can create an emotional climate in the household that constitutes psychological abuse and neglect in its own right. What is more, about 1.2 million children are themselves abused physically or sexually within their families. It's no surprise that many children feel unsafe at home.

But this is not the whole story, nor is it the main point of this chapter. Children from violence-free homes confront danger once they leave the safety of their apartment building or front yard. A third of the children in some inner-city, high-crime neighborhoods have witnessed a homicide by age 15. A 6-year-old girl in such a neighborhood once told us that her job was to find her 2-year-old sister whenever the shooting started and get her to safety in the bathtub of their apartment. "The bathroom is the safest place," she said. Being responsible for the safety of another, younger child is too big a responsibility for a 6-year-old girl.

For other children, the basis for their insecurity is not life in the urban war zone but just life. A national survey conducted by *Newsweek* and the Children's Defense Fund in 1993 found that only a minority of children nationwide said they felt "very safe" once they walked out the door; most said they only felt "somewhat safe," and about 12 percent said they felt "unsafe." A Harris poll of sixth- to twelfth-graders in 1992 revealed that 35 percent worried they would not live to old age because they would be shot. In 1999, 52 percent of America's 13- to 17-year-olds said they thought what happened at Columbine High School could happen in their school.

The big story in recent years has been the spread of this fear and insecurity to more and more children, those beyond the urban war zone, children who are not poor. Why are even youngsters in small towns and suburbs afraid? Why are even economically secure children afraid? Why do so many children and their parents feel they are under siege?

Insecurity Spreads

More and more children in the United States are experiencing a growing sense of insecurity about the world inside and outside the boundaries of their families. As the news media devote ever more coverage to the dangers of life, it is not surprising that children are worried. For one thing, they are preoccupied with kidnapping. Teacher after teacher tells us that if he or she asks students what they worry about, kidnapping looms large for most. A study conducted by pediatricians in Ohio reported that 43 percent of the elementary school children studied thought it was likely they would be kidnapped by a stranger, despite the fact that the odds of a child actually being kidnapped by a stranger are minute (about one in a million). Having been bombarded with messages of threat via the news and their worried parents and other well-meaning adults, kids draw the logical conclusion: If the adults are so scared, maybe I should be too.

Children tend to mirror the responses of key adults in their lives. Calm and confident parents and teachers tend to produce confident children who believe the world is manageable. We have seen this theme play itself out around the world, and it is well documented by child psychologists and researchers everywhere. This finding highlights the importance of family and school in creating or undermining a child's sense of security. And it speaks volumes about why parents must cultivate a mindful calm that can reassure their children and make them authentically safer.

Kids are concerned about family dissolution. To children, security equates with stability. Many children ask their parents, "When are you getting divorced?" When, not if. They seem to assume that divorce is inevitable, a sword of Damocles hanging over their heads. The demographics justify their concern. Census Bureau data continue to document a divorce rate of about 50 percent. When fears for physical safety are added to a family's instability, the net result is a growing sense of insecurity among our children.

Television presents a world full of threat. In general, the more television you watch, the more paranoid your view of the community around you. We discussed this once with a woman who manages a high-rise housing unit for the elderly. "That explains a lot," she said. "The old people in my building do two things: sit in their rooms watching TV and come down to the lobby to talk about how scared they are to go out!" Old and young are the most vulnerable. American kids watch a lot of television, most of it adult television. The level of predatory behavior on television is very high: maniacs, killers, and kidnappers abound. It is no wonder that so many children and parents feel the world is against them.

Remember that whether it's real life or television imagery, it doesn't take much violence and terror to set a tone of menace. Even in the worst war zones, shooting and killing are intermittent. In the worst high-crime neighborhood, it only takes shots fired a few times per month and homicides a few times a year to create a year-round climate of danger, to establish insecurity as a dominant psychological reality. In these situations children may live with low-level Post-Traumatic Stress Disorder and hypervigilance as a condition of life. Memory of the emotions of trauma does not decay; it remains fresh. Once you have the feeling of danger, it takes very little new threat to sustain it. For most children in the United States, the world is not as violent as they think it is. But their fear is real, and to some degree grounded in reality as they see it. Their social maps are colored with fear.

American kids are little anthropologists as they watch and listen to what goes on around them. What are they learning from the news, from their favorite television programs, from cartoons, from current-events lessons at school, from watching and listening to their parents and aunts and uncles and grandparents? What are they learning about the world? We think that, more and more, they are learning that the world is a very dangerous place.

The World Can Be a Dangerous Place

Some years ago we did a "ride along" with a couple of tough police officers in Philadelphia. At the end of a frustrating day of tracking down lawbreakers, the two officers did catch a drug dealer in the act and brought him in for processing. While waiting in the detention center as the suspect was booked, we asked the police officer if he thought all this arresting did any good. He replied, "No." "What would it take to make a difference?" we asked him. He smiled, formed his right hand into a gun and said, "If I could shoot them as I caught them."

We thought of this police officer often as we sat listening to the life stories of incarcerated teenagers, kids in jail for violent crimes. As we listened to the stories, we were deeply moved and troubled by what we heard and what we saw on the young faces of these boys, we who ourselves are parents of teenagers. Like the policeman who wanted to solve the drug problem by shooting the dealers as he caught them, each of these teenagers in his own way testified to the problem of violence in the lives of American kids—particularly American boys.

Americans accept violence as a strategy for punishment, a way of dealing with conflict, and a form of entertainment. All this is evident in what incarcerated teenagers have to say. Each of them is a living, breathing illustration of how vulnerable kids have succumbed to being slowly poisoned in their own homes and communities.

When asked why they carry guns, many boys in prison say they were scared and carrying a gun made them feel safer and more powerful. When we asked a 9-year-old boy in a California housing project what it would take to make him feel safer there, his only response was, "If I had a gun of my own." On February 29, 2000, a 6-year-old boy in Flint, Michigan, shot and killed a 6-year-old girl in his school. A few weeks later a 12-year-old boy in Ohio brought a gun to school to demand that he be reunited with his imprisoned mother.

The problem of violence in our society is pervasive in scope and cancerous in nature. It infects our institutional life, our community life, and drives the dark side of our culture. It has become an inescapable and influential factor in understanding childhood in America. We get used to it. We adjust. We lower our expectations.

Imagine asking fish to describe water. How could they explain their surroundings, when water is all they have ever known? So it is with adults and youth today. Unless we can travel to other places where peace and calm are the cultural norms, we may never notice the ubiquity of violence around us. During a meeting at a school for emotionally disturbed kids, we asked one of the teachers how she felt when one of the boys raised his fist to her. At first she looked puzzled, as if she didn't remember the incident, which had occurred only that morning. Then the light of recognition dawned. "I guess I didn't notice it," she said. "You get used to it when it happens all the time."

Safety flows from a feeling of security. Of course, we as adults know that there is danger in the world. We know that there is cancer, that there are serial killers loose among us, that horrible things happen every day. But we also know that children need childhood. They need to be sheltered from the dark side of life until they have grown strong enough to recognize it and not be traumatized by it. When adult society is working well, we conspire to keep some dark secrets from children, because we owe them that innocence. We can pay special attention to three dark secrets.

Snowden's Secret

The first of these three secrets we call *Snowden's Secret.* Our reference is Joseph Heller's book *Catch-22,* which tells the story of American bomber crews during World War II. The central character, Yossarian, has undergone a traumatic experience, learning what he calls Snowden's secret. During one of his plane's missions, Yossarian receives a message over the intercom that another member of the crew, Snowden, has been hit by antiaircraft fire. When he goes to help Snowden and opens his flak jacket, Snowden's insides fall out on the floor.

This is Snowden's Secret—that is, the human body, which

appears so firm and durable, is really only a fragile bag filled with gooey stuff and lumps, suspended precariously on a very fragile skeleton. Violence reveals this secret, and it is a traumatic experience "from which you never fully recover." It requires all of your emotional, spiritual, and philosophical resources to cope with Snowden's Secret, as people who work in emergency rooms or who investigate automobile crashes or who travel to war zones will attest.

Children learn Snowden's Secret from experiencing—particularly, witnessing—violence, when the human body meets bullets and knives. And this witnessing need not be firsthand. When we traveled to Kuwait at the end of the Gulf War on behalf of UNICEF, we interviewed kids who had learned Snowden's Secret firsthand. They had seen atrocities—shootings, hangings, beatings—and some of them had unwittingly brought violent trauma upon themselves—like the boys we met who had been playing with a hand grenade until it exploded and tore open the chest of their cousin. Many of these children were experiencing Post-Traumatic Stress Disorder.

That these youngsters were traumatized was no surprise. What *was* surprising was that a year later, when more systematic follow-up research was conducted, another group of Kuwaiti children was identified as demonstrating trauma symptoms. They had not witnessed atrocities firsthand; they had been shown videotapes of Iraqi atrocities in an effort to indoctrinate them politically about the origins and meaning of the Iraqi invasion. And seeing the atrocities on video had an unfortunate side effect: They had learned Snowden's Secret by remote control.

The Kuwaiti children came to mind when we visited a first-grade classroom in Chicago. A little girl—Gloria—brought up a little handmade book she had written for the class's "author's project." This Birthday Book began nicely enough: "Happy Birthday" read the first page. But then began a visual litany of all the reasons why children *didn't* have birthdays: because they were shot, because they were stabbed, because they were beheaded, because they were disemboweled, because they were kidnapped. It made you wonder about the source of this flood of traumatic images. What had happened to this little girl that she should tell this story?

After some investigation, it became clear what had happened. When her mother went out, she left Gloria in the care of her teenage cousins, who sat her down in front of their favorite movies, *Nightmare on Elm Street, Halloween,* and the other slasher films that are so popular with American adolescents. But for Gloria, these films—and the image of Freddy Krueger in particular—were traumatic. She was learning Snowden's Secret from an expert. If one were trying to design a character specifically for the purpose of traumatizing young children, Freddy Krueger would be nearly ideal. He can't be killed, so he always comes back. He enters into the dreams of his victims, so you can't protect yourself by asserting the distinction between fantasy and reality. And he kills in a particularly vivid manner, with the finger knives that adorn his hands.

Informal surveys indicate a substantial proportion of young children know Freddy Krueger. Several years ago an informal survey conducted by a Chicago police officer reported that 15 percent of first graders reported having seen at least one of his movies. Whenever we went into elementary school classrooms at that time, we found he was well known. The same police officer in Chicago reported that he had done a survey of eighth graders and found that 85 percent said they had recently been to see an R-rated violent movie, and further, that 55 percent of the time they were accompanied by a younger child. From our perspective, teaching kids about Snowden's Secret through movies like *Nightmare on Elm Street* is like teaching sex education by showing kids hard-core pornography. Learning Snowden's Secret is a threat to children, one that this mode of instruction compounds. But Snowden's is only one of the secrets children learn from witnessing violence. There is another secret, perhaps even more disturbing.

Dantrell's Secret

Dantrell Davis was the little boy who lived in Chicago until he was shot to death on his way to school in 1992. As we reported in Chapter 1, as he walked the 75 feet between his mother and the school, where his teachers awaited, he was shot in the back of the head and killed. His death sends an important message to other children: Adults can't protect you; you are on your own. And it is a message that many children—perhaps, most children today—learn as they watch television programs and go to movies that hammer away at this theme of vulnerability.

If Snowden's Secret teaches children something disturbing about the human body, Dantrell's Secret teaches them something at least equally disturbing about the social fabric, and about adult authority in particular. It teaches children that you may be left alone in the face of threat. Alone.

One of the truisms of research on children growing up in war zones around the world is that the first line of defense against fear and trauma is parental protection. As one observer put it after examining children in England during World War II, "Children measure the danger that threatens them chiefly by the reactions of those around them, especially by their trusted parents and teachers." This has certainly been our experience while traveling to a dozen war zones in the last decade.

Children enter into a social contract with adults. The terms of this contract are roughly these: I will obey and trust you, and in return you will protect and care for me. Dantrell's Secret voids this contract. One little boy we visited who lived in a refugee camp had learned Dantrell's Secret. Soldiers had come into the camp looking for someone. With the boy's mother standing next to him, a soldier grabbed the boy and put a knife to his throat. "Tell me where Omar is," he said to the mother, "or I'll cut your boy's throat." The fact that this could happen to him while his mother stood powerless was the most traumatic element of the experience.

Beyond such dramatic incidents are situations in which it is the corrosive effects of parental depression—especially maternal depression—that are the source of the problem. Living with depressed mothers has some predictable consequences for children, particularly when it occurs in a context filled with other risk factors, like poverty, an absent father, or substance abuse. Children of depressed mothers in such high-risk situations tend to receive inadequate adult supervision, and thus are more likely to be injured in accidents.

Millions of children in America face similarly depressed mothers. A research group in New Orleans led by psychologist Joy Osofsky conducted a mental health survey in a public housing project like Dantrell's, and they discovered that 50 percent of the mothers were seriously depressed. They also found that 40 percent of the mother-child attachment relationships in the first year of life were disrupted ("disorganized," to use the investigators' term). This means that these children would likely be less resilient in dealing with their high-risk, low-opportunity social environment.

More and more children are living with parents who feel overwhelmed by the world they see on television, in the newspapers, and outside their front doors. Without parents being actively in charge, children learn Dantrell's Secret and have it reinforced daily. And what do these children do to cope with this knowledge? How do they adapt to their feeling that they have to fend for themselves, that they are on their own in a dangerous environment? They cope as best they can, and this includes banding together in gangs for protection. As a boy in

Michigan once told us, "If I join a gang, I'm 50 percent safe. If I don't join a gang, I'm zero percent safe." Adults just don't figure into the equation. That's a conclusion too many kids today are reaching.

For many parents, it feels as though they are facing these dangers alone. Particularly for parents whose children are temperamentally difficult or behaviorally impossible, it often seems as if the community lets them down. This feeling of being let down often focuses on the school.

Here's what one parent told us about her frustration with her child's school as an ally:

> When you start knowing what your kids are really doing, it becomes hard to trust them. Schoolwise, he is failing. Big time. He had to repeat ninth grade, and he is in tenth currently, and he is just not doing anything. I started getting notes from the principal's office: "Eric skips his classes." "Eric isn't at school." "Did he come to school?" I'm on the phone with the attendance office all the time. They would call me to say, "Do you know where Eric is?" It got to a point where I said, "I put him on the school bus this morning. I know he went to school. Why doesn't the school know where he is?" The attendance office would tell me that they can't keep track of where all 1,500 students are at all times. It became very discouraging. What was I expected to do? I can make sure he is up, dressed and fed in the morning and that he gets on the school bus, but I can't walk him by the hand to his classes. If the school could not keep track of his whereabouts even when he was in the school, how could I? I don't know. I don't understand how this system is supposed to work anymore. When I was growing up, I didn't know what I was going to be, but I knew I had to go to school. Kids today, they have no clue what they're going to do. I see that in my son. And they get unmotivated, then they get to school,

where the size of the building and the number of students makes it easy to skip, and they just go off and "hang out" and come home after school. If your kid is motivated, then he'll go to school even if it is big. But if you have the misfortune of having a kid who lacks motivation to do the work, you're left out to dry. All the school does is call home and issue warnings, and eventually their "solution" is to have the kid suspended, and if that doesn't work to have him expelled. I think they are trying, but they are losing the battle. They are low on options.

Milgram's Secret

The third secret learned by children exposed to traumatic violence is what we call Milgram's Secret. The reference here is to psychologist Stanley Milgram's research in the late 1950s and early 1960s on the willingness of normal adults to inflict torture on others if they are ordered to do so or if they believe there is some other justification. Before he conducted his research, Miligram asked samples of adults if they thought normal young adults were capable of sadistic behavior against defenseless victims. The respondents overwhelmingly replied, "It is not possible." Then Milgram did studies and found that most people were wrong. The subjects in his study were quite capable of inflicting horrible pain and suffering if he ordered them to do so. It was possible.

Milgram's Secret is that when it comes to violence, anything is possible. An adult survivor of child abuse once reported the following incident. The police were called once when she was a child to investigate reports that her mother was beating her. When the police interviewed the child, she denied that her mother beat her. Later, her mother asked her why she didn't tell the police about the beating. She looked at her mother and said,

"Because you could kill me." Milgram's Secret: *Anything* is possible. Children learn it, and we are all jeopardized by that learning.

Children learn this lesson from watching television and going to the movies, where producers, writers, and directors compete to portray ever-more ingenious and despicable demonstrations of Milgram's Secret. How many ways are there to kill and maim? The mass media seems determined to find out. Is there any form of mutilation that is out of bounds and beyond human possibility? Survivors of Nazi death camps, the Pol Pot Khmer Rouge terror in Cambodia, and all the individual serial killers of the world know that the answer is no. Now children and youth will know, too.

In the post-Columbine era, parents and professionals must confront another dimension of Milgram's Secret: Any threat made to or by a child can end in lethal violence. Here's what a mother told us about what has been happening to her 12-year-old son Peter. She tells us:

> I'm not sure that what's happening is typical adolescent behavior of teasing and picking-on, or something that's indicative of something more scary. I don't want to overreact, but since my child is apparently a target of some violent language, I also don't want to ignore the situation. Last semester I learned that my son was the target of what I would term "stalking" from a peer. He followed him around in school, stared him down in shared classes, made comments about "getting you," and kept a daily log of his activities (what he was wearing, who he interacted with, where he lived, etc.). It was rumored that he had created a Web page titled "10 Ways to Kill Peter," but we were never able to prove it was more than a rumor. We sought the intervention of the school; spoke with the perpetrator's mother, who classified her son as "difficult in social situations; doesn't make friends easily"; and

felt confident that appropriate actions had taken place on the part of school authorities. Yesterday we received another report from school that another child, whom we've learned is part of a group that hangs out with the original perpetrator, wrote an essay for a class assignment that indicated he wanted to kill my son and his good friend. The fact that he is linked to this first child makes me view what could, under other circumstances, simply be a kid spouting anger and nothing more, as something much more serious. Again, I understood the point you made about the "hysteria" surrounding the school shootings of late, and the fact that in general, schools are more safe than ever. *But,* I'm wondering whether there are too many little pieces that have scary implications to ignore.

When we met with her, she was struggling to decide how seriously to take the threats. Then that 6-year-old boy in Flint, Michigan, brought a gun to school and killed a classmate to avenge a conflict the two children had engaged in the day before. Now this mother knows Milgram's Secret: Anything is possible. Her son's tormentor really could deliver on his threats. It's statistically unlikely, of course. But statistics are not reassuring to a parent watching television news. This mother is demanding that her son's school do more than just hope for the best. When learned together, Snowden's, Dantrell's, and Milgram's secrets offer a potent recipe for personal and social destruction, and one that speaks loudly about the children's interior experience of violence and trauma.

The Costs of Adjusting to Violent Trauma

Early exposure to violent trauma can also make kids prime candidates for involvement in gangs, where the economy of the illicit drug trade offers a sense of belonging and solidarity as well as danger. Violent trauma reduces a child's confidence that he or she will survive into old age, with the result being that children and youth have diminished prospects for the future.

Child psychiatrist Lenore Terr studied a group of children kidnapped and held hostage in a frightening underground storage facility. This became known as the Chowchilla Kidnapping. The kids eventually escaped, and the perpetrators were arrested and sent to prison. Nonetheless, a year later there was a significant six-year decrease in what the children expected their life span to be.

At the extreme, this may lead to terminal thinking. This is evident when you ask a 15-year-old what he expects to be when he is 30 and he answers, "Dead." But many kids beyond the most severely traumatized develop milder symptoms along these lines. Lack of a positive future orientation can produce depression, rage, and disregard for human life—their own and others'. It also undermines motivation to participate in the investment activities of adolescence, such as staying in school, doing homework, and avoiding high-risk behaviors such as unprotected sex, carrying weapons, and participating in the drug trade.

From our perspective, the most important consequence of living with violence is that it has an impact on the values of children and youth. Beyond terminal thinking there is juvenile vigilantism. When children learn that they cannot rely upon adults to protect them, they are likely to turn to their peers and to rely upon themselves. No kid wants to feel afraid, and they will do what it takes to change that situation. If it means joining a gang, so be it. If it means carrying a gun, so be it. If it means talking tough and adopting a tough, nasty facade, so be it. Almost anything is better than being afraid all the time.

Research gathered by the National Research Council in its 1993 book *Understanding and Preventing Violence* indicates that patterns of aggression are so well established by age 8 that without intervention they then begin to predict patterns of aggression at age 38. Psychologist Leonard Eron and his colleagues, found that the same kids who are named by the peers at age 8 as the kids who hit and push and bully and shove and kick and bite and fight, typically become the adults who hit members of their family, get into fights in the community, and drive their cars aggressively. Not all do, of course, but the link is there. And values play a role in all this.

Psychologist Stephen Asher has studied the "legitimization of aggression" among elementary school children. He found that the more kids agree with statements validating aggression—such as "It's OK to hit people if they hurt your feelings" and "It's OK to hit people if they hurt you"—the more aggressive they are in the classroom, on the school yard, on the playground, and in the neighborhood. Unless we reach them with healing experiences and offer them a moral and political framework within which to process their experiences, kids are likely to be drawn to values and ideologies that legitimatize and reward their aggression, their rage, their fear, and the hateful cynicism that they feed upon in our culture.

The medieval political philosopher Machiavelli wrote his cynical political tract *The Prince* soon after being imprisoned and abused by the government of his city. Traumatic experiences create a fertile field for nasty political and religious beliefs and organizations. The personal histories of terrorists, religious fanatics, gangsters, killers and authoritarian bigots often reveal a similar pattern that combines traumatic experiences of violence coupled with social exploitation and oppression. These individuals are the canaries who tell us how bad the social toxins are in the environment. Others show the milder variants that, because of fortuitous family experiences or special individual resilience or effective professional intervention, do not deteriorate into full-blown criminal violence in the home, on the streets, or in the workplace.

On the whole, the links are forged early. If we don't disengage these links immediately, we are likely to witness adolescent aggression that becomes the stuff of which serious criminal violence is made. And if things get that far, it may take years, even decades, in a closely controlled environment to accomplish the twofold task of protection and rehabilitation. It may take all this to accomplish the kind of transformation that is necessary to overcome a personal legacy of traumatic violence.

In general, it is only the most vulnerable among our children who display fully the bitter fruits of living in a violent society. But even if these kids do not live in your home, chances are, your children go to school with them. Is it any wonder that more than half of the 13- to 17-year-olds in our country surveyed in 1999 thought that what happened in Littleton, Colorado, could happen in their school. Each year the number of vulnerable children, youth, families, and communities grows. Each year the level of social toxicity associated with violence and trauma increases.

There is enough reality to these fears to feed the fear and paranoia of children. As in the case of childhood kidnapping, where the actual odds of it happening to a particular child are very, very low, we need to find ways to communicate confidence to children and the message that we the adults are taking responsibility for keeping them safe. In both cases, there is a role for kids to play, but it is mainly one of communicating information to adults rather than doing the direct work of intervention.

At the extreme, the role of peers in youth violence is horrifying. A *New York Times* study of American mass murderers found only one major difference between adults and teens who engage in rampage or serial killing. While adults who do so are classic loners, teens who do so typically have active peer support. At its worst, this can take the form of a psychiatric condition known as Shared Psychotic Disorder, in which the distorted thinking and feeling of a clinically disturbed child draws in a second, otherwise "normal" child. When the second child is highly attached to or perhaps dependent upon the first, he (or she) can come to share the distorted thinking and feeling of the other child. Together, then, they form a delusional world in which mass murder may make perfect sense, as it did to Eric Harris and Dylan Klebold.

Conclusion

There is danger out there—and sometimes inside too. Some children live in violent homes. Some neighborhoods are physically dangerous—with many children having firsthand encounters with violence on the streets and the playgrounds. Many children must contend with racism and homophobia. Most children live in a society in which they feel afraid of strangers. All this poses a challenge to parents who must find a way to promote the safety of their children without inducing paranoia.

What to do? We believe the starting point is to recognize that a defeatist attitude is the surest path to defeat. Psychologist Nick Stennet and his colleagues have spent years studying strong families, families that endure in the face of adversity and which succeed in helping children and youth make the transition to adulthood successfully. One of their conclusions is that such families have the ability to deal with crises in a positive manner. Studies of resilience reveal that one of the foundations for successful coping is an active, positive approach to the world. Anthropologist Dan Sheinfeld found that children whose parents communicated a message of powerlessness and retreat in the face of urban danger were less successful than parents who told their children they could master the environment no matter how dangerous. We will return to the "how to" in Chapter 7, but here we can conclude with the basic lesson of all these studies.

Lesson: Safety begins at home in the social maps of children, but it does not end there, for children rely upon all the adults in their world to teach confidence, not fear.

5

Our Children's
Secret Lives

Keeping Secrets

Infants are the embodiment of innocence. They keep no secrets. They tell no lies. But over time, that changes. As children develop the intellectual competence to recognize the difference between what is reality and what is fantasy, the world of truth telling changes for them—and for us as parents. At some point, we as children realize that our parents are not all-knowing. It dawns on us fairly early that it is possible to influence what our parents know about our actions and thoughts. We become aware that it is possible to conceal something and get away with it, or at least try. As we get into our teens, we learn that information is power, and that to successfully conceal information makes us feel powerful. It may make us feel guilty, or upset, but the sense

97

of power behind a successful lie is tangible. It gives us a sense of control over our environment and the people in it. It also gives us a sense of influence over our fate, as in "If I don't reveal the truth of my wrongdoing, I will not be punished" kind of thinking. Lying and truth telling have powerful consequences, and the drive to gain control of the consequences by hiding the truth is something that manifests early in life.

In their important book on children's credibility in the context of courtroom testimonies, psychologists Stephen Ceci and Maggie Bruck devote an entire section to the issue of lying and truth telling in children. They explain that historically, most people thought young children were incapable of lying because it was believed they did not yet have the intellectual capacity to do so. Even in the early decades of the twentieth century, pioneering child development psychologist Jean Piaget assumed that lying requires a kind of intellectual sophistication that children simply do not have. There are many adults today who still refuse to believe a young child is capable of lying. But as child psychology research advanced, new evidence showed that even very young children sometimes do lie, and that they can do so fully appreciating that they are giving differing stories to their listeners.

But even with the intellectual ability to do so, why would a child lie? Research in recent decades has focused on five particular motivations to lie or tell the truth: 1) to avoid punishment, 2) to keep a game going, 3) to keep a promise (e.g., "This will be our secret"), 4) to gain something personally, and 5) to avoid being embarrassed. The bottom line: children will lie about events when they have sufficient reason to gain something from lying. Parents already know that adults lie, which makes lying a concept that adults can easily relate to. After all, who among us never, ever lies? But parents have a more difficult time accepting the concept that children lie. And when it comes to their own children, the ability for most parents to accept this fact is even more limited. "My child would not lie to me. I know him." "I would know if she lied to me." How often have we heard ourselves say this to a principal, a neighbor or an in-law? We defend our children's honesty until the bitter end. We want so much to extend the days of childhood innocence for as long as possible, until all proof to the contrary has been established. For some parents, the desire to believe that their children don't keep big secrets from them can lead to a rude awakening.

Here is an example of how hiding the truth manifests early. A 4-year-old boy is feeding his lunch to the family dog, against the house rules, while his mother walks down to the basement to put some clothes in the dryer. After he is finished, his mother returns into the room and, seeing his empty plate, congratulates him on eating his whole lunch. He realizes that she does not know he fed his sandwich to the dog, *and* that if he does not tell her she will never know. He does not volunteer. He pretends he ate the sandwich. He fools his mother. This capacity to pretend offers the child a rich world of make believe and fantasy play. This is wonderful. But it also offers the child the option of a secret life, experiences, thoughts and feelings unknown to the parent.

At first children may be clumsy about using this newfound ability to pretend and misrepresent themselves. A 5-year-old boy is playing with a toy truck in the living room and accidentally knocks a vase off the table. The child stands next to a broken vase, with the offending toy in hand, but when the parent asks, "Did you break the vase?" the child replies, "No, I didn't do it." A girl in a first-grade classroom wets herself in class. When the teacher asked what happened, she replies, "My shoe leaked." A 4-year-old tells his parents, "I'm not Joey anymore; I'm Janey and I am a teenager."

These early experiences with deception set the stage for a long process of learning to differentiate truth from fiction, the motivation to tell the truth, and the savvy to know all the social conventions about when not telling the truth is acceptable ("white lies"). But it also establishes the foundation for the child to have a secret life, a life apart from what parents know. Some of this secret life may concern socially unacceptable feelings (for example, "I hate my baby sister!"). Some of it may concern violation of parental rules (for example, "I hid candy under my pillow to eat after the lights were out"). This is the stuff of childhood. But in adolescence the stakes may increase dramatically.

Suppose you were to ask a group of 18- to 19-year-olds if they ever thought about killing people. What do you think the results would be? Psychologist Peter Crabb did that with a group of Penn State students, with shocking results: Some 60 percent of the males said they had had a recent fantasy of killing someone, while 32 percent of the females had as well.

Journalist Patricia Hersch spent six years doing research for a book about teenagers, *A Tribe Apart: A Journey into the Heart of American Adolescence.* What did she learn? "Today's teens are a tribe apart. The most striking characteristic of many adolescents today is their aloneness. . . . I've learned how much their world eludes us adults—not necessarily because they are rebelling or evading us, but because we are not part of it. . . . That freedom changes everything for kids."

She concludes: "There have always been troubled kids. But today their increased isolation allows pressures to build up with no release, no guidance. There is often little monitoring of how adolescents spend their time, whether it be on the Internet, with video games, music, building bombs or doing their homework." This isolation—or perhaps more accurately, this *self-*isolation—is the foundation for the secret life of teenagers. Even teenagers who are blessed to have a family and extended family—many of them loving, caring and vigilant—can create an island of isolation within this life, where caring adults surround them. This secret life can exist in different forms and degrees, and it can take its darkest form in the life and death of a boy like Dylan Klebold, who hid his troubled inner life and behavior from his parents until April 20, 1999.

Even as our children grow into adolescence, we want so much to believe that our kids are coming clean with us, or that if they were to hide major information, we would somehow be able to tell. This belief probably runs even more deeply in families where parents consider themselves emotionally close and well connected to their kids. Families where one or both parents involve and invest themselves in their teenagers' lives pride themselves, justifiably so, on the quality of their family values, including honesty and a sense of openness in communicating with their teens. When kids are doing well, at school and seemingly all around, occasional drifts and problems are assumed to be part of growing pains, and overall, confidence is high that all is relatively well with their adolescent children. Yet even in well-functioning families, adolescents manage to keep certain pieces of important information from their unsuspecting parents. The degree of severity of secrets kept by teens varies from family to family, of course, but even the most vigilant parent may be shocked to learn just how widespread deep secrets are among teens.

When asked: "Did your parents know about everything you did when you were a teenager that was dangerous or dishonest?" most of us would answer "no." And we can assume that today's teenagers are not telling their parents everything either. The question, though, is "*What* aren't they telling their parents?" To test this out, we gave a questionnaire to first-year undergraduate students at Cornell University, an Ivy League college where our surveyed students predominantly come from two-parent families of means. The results indicate, not surprisingly, that many of the students had some secret life of which their parents were, almost by definition, unaware. What did surprise us, however, is the seriousness of some of the events these students kept from their parents throughout their teens and until then, even though the vast majority of these students were living in families with intact marriages, where both parents were present and involved in their children's lives. The point being that, even in families where conditions were good for maintaining a healthy level of supervision of teens, teens still managed to keep dramatic events in their lives from ever reaching their parents' consciousness.

We asked 275 first-year undergraduate students to describe the "worst thing, in the sense of most dangerous or troubling" that they had taken part in as a teenager in high school, but that their "parents never found out about." Here are some of the answers we received: 18 percent said they had "stolen from their parents," with 65 percent of the parents whose kids stole from them never finding out. Fourteen percent of the students were "arrested or detained," and 27 percent of the parents of those kids never found out. Forty-eight percent said they went to web sites prohibited to minors, a fact 85 percent of their parents were unaware of. Twenty-three percent admitted to driving under the influence, but a whopping 94 percent of their parents still do not know. Eleven percent said they used hard drugs such as cocaine and/or ecstasy, unbeknownst to 92 percent of their parents. One quarter of the students sadly reported that they considered suicide, and 87 percent of the parents of those teens never knew. One male student said he actually attempted suicide and was able to keep that from his parents. Of the eight female students who also attempted suicide, nearly half of their parents still do not know.

When asked to elaborate on some of their secrets, students provided the following explanations:

"I thought a lot about death. I thought about suicide, but after much thought I decided that was morally wrong and I couldn't do it, even if I really wanted to. I often prayed that perhaps I'd be in an accident or something similar, so that way I could escape from my abusive father."

"I told my parents that I was sleeping at a friend's house, then went to a boyfriend's, where we drank and did cocaine. When I got home the next morning, my mom was upset because she had called the friend's house and found out I was not there. So I proceeded to make up another lie about where I had been, and she believed me."

"I was involved in a situation over a girl that escalated to the point that myself and my best friend were threatened with being shot by a guy who had an interest in this girl."

"One night when I was 17, my friends and I went to a hotel party where most of the guys were at least 22 or 23. There was a lot of drinking, and I was pressured to take shots of whiskey until I passed out. Then someone got my friends to leave the room. When one of my friends forced her way back into the room, she found this guy having sex with me while I was unconscious."

"I drank almost every weekend of my senior year in high school, and my parents had no idea. On one occasion I almost died due to my impaired (drunken) judgment. I was so drunk I jumped on the front end of a car full of my friends, and the car drove off down the bumpy road. After a while I slid off the front of the car and landed in front on the wheels. I heard the brakes squeal and when the car stopped, the right tire was flush against my ribs. I couldn't even get up until the car rolled back because my sweater was still caught under the wheel."

"I vandalized the home of an enemy with a few friends, causing thousands of dollars' worth of damage. After perpetrating the crime, I eluded the police who pursued us as we split up leaving the scene of the crime. Fortunately, the cops did not get a good look at us and were unable to track us down after we fled."

"There are too many for there to be a 'worst.' I had unprotected sex with my boyfriend when I was 14 and thought I was pregnant when my period was late. I was seriously depressed and contemplated suicide. I hung out with drug dealers."

"A group of us broke into an old school during one winter on weekends so we could have keg parties. We vandalized the school and tore up countless records and important documents that were being stored there. Eventually, the police found out but my parents never did."

"Here's a list of happenings they never knew (and still don't know about): being raped, using drugs to cope, being mugged, dealing drugs, joining a gang, my friends' overdoses, a close friend's suicide, abusive boyfriends."

"I had frequent unprotected sex with male friends, and worse still, I smoked pot just about every day junior and senior year. My social life revolved around getting high."

"I seriously contemplated suicide for most of my high school years. Also, I often cut and hurt myself during high school as a way to transfer the emotional pain to physical pain, and probably also as an attempt to get their attention from the scars and bruises. They never noticed."

"I did cocaine. To this day I don't think I would ever admit to my parents that I have done cocaine, and certainly not how often I used to do it. My fear is that it would forever change how they think of me and make them worry."

"I considered suicide in high school. My parents never knew. I was diagnosed as manic-depressive my senior year of high school, which had manifested itself through an eating disorder. In retrospect, I can see that my bipolar disorder had been building since approximately 12 years of age. I was very smart and knew that there was something abnormal in my behavior. I used my intelligence to hide it."

These are academically successful young people (more than three quarters are girls), responsible and bright enough to succeed in a prestigious elite university, and majoring in human development. If these highly functioning students have a secret life, then what can we expect of less fortunate, more troubled kids? Here is some of what we can expect. One boy we interviewed in prison reports that he had twenty-two guns hidden in the basement of his family's home, and his mother and father never suspected until after he was arrested for selling guns to other kids. A girl we talked to went to her church's youth group meeting every Sunday evening, and then on the way home often stopped off with some friends to have sex and take drugs. Her parents found out only years later, when she told them about it the night before her wedding.

Why Don't Parents Know?

"Parents must be held responsible. They should have known what their children were involved in." What is the problem here? Is it a lack of parental monitoring? Certainly many people would answer "yes." There is a strong belief in our society *at least among adults,* that parents who really want to know what their kids are doing will know. This naturally leads to the conclusion that parents who don't know either don't want to know or are negligent in taking the steps necessary to find out what their kids are doing.

What about something as horrible as the Columbine school shootings. While it seems many adults are quick to blame the Klebold and Harris parents, protesting that "they must have known," the students we asked disagreed. We posed this question to the students: "Do you think it is possible for a teenager to be planning such an attack without the parents knowing about it?" The result: 99 percent said "yes." Here are a few sample comments:

"Parents only see what they want to see or what their children allow them to see."

"For one thing, parents tend to idealize their children. Also, it is impossible to know everything. A teenager can hide many things, and if parents have no reason to suspect maladaptive behavior, they won't have reason to question their child."

"Teenagers can be amazingly adept at hiding their lives from their parents."

"Certain people are able to show one personality on the outside or in front of family, and be someone else underneath and around friends."

Results of a recent study by Swedish psychologists Mary Margaret Kerr and Hakan Stattin convey an important message about the reality behind parental "monitoring": *The quality of a parent's monitoring depends on how much a child/teen discloses to the parent.* In other words, *it is not so much what parents do, but what their kids tell them about.* Viewed in this light, teenagers' secret lives seriously compromise the parents' ability to do their job well. Their report is entitled "What Parents Know, How They Know it, and Several Forms of Adolescent Adjustment."

Kerr and Stattin studied over a thousand 14-year-olds and their parents. They did find that the more parents knew about what their kids did, the better adjusted those kids were—less delinquent, fewer school problems, less depression, more positive expectations of life, more positive peers, and better relations with parents. It sounds like an endorsement of the popular belief that parents who monitor have better kids. However, that is not the whole story.

Kerr and Stattin found that the spontaneous disclosure of information by children explained more of what was really happening in their kids' lives than the efforts of parents to track and monitor their kids. "These findings suggest that the term 'monitoring' is a misnomer if it is used to refer to parental knowledge, because the process by which parents get knowledge (about what their children are into) is more an activity of children than of parents." In other words, we blame parents for not properly monitoring their children, without understanding that in reality, we as parents can do only so much to monitor. If the child is not willing to let the parents in on what he or she is doing, and especially if the child is skilled at concealing and hiding, the parents' efforts cannot be effective.

To make matters worse, we are told that the *better-adjusted* kids apparently tell more to their parents about what they are doing than do the *less-well-adjusted* kids. They conclude: "There is no direct evidence to link parents' tracking efforts with good adolescent adjustment" (p. 373). "In other words, in spite of what the label implies, parental 'monitoring' represented child disclosure more than parental tracking and surveillance, and child disclosure was the primary link to low norm-breaking." The more your children tell you, the more successful you will be as a parent—not the extra amount of your effort to try to monitor them. If you have the misfortune of having a child who does not readily disclose information, your overall ability to be a "good" parent will be compromised, because tracking and surveilling our children does not succeed if our children conceal information from us. Therefore, parenting children who have secret lives becomes a very difficult task, analogous to trying to control a reflection on the wall when the object is actually hiding behind the screen. We see the image, it looks like the object, but the real story is going on somewhere else.

Kerr and Stattin also tell us that kids who feel that their parents are trying to control them have worse adjustments than kids who feel their parents trust them. Remember, that this is a study of 14-year-olds. By that age, parents and kids have developed a lot of momentum; there is a history to their patterns of relating. Some kids have established a momentum of positive behavior, and their parents rightfully trust them (and these kids freely disclose what they are doing). Other kids have established a pattern of negative behavior, and their parents are rightfully suspicious (and seek to control these out-of-control kids).

Remember that for the most part, adolescence is the culmination, the coming to fruition, of childhood patterns, not some dramatically discrepant period of life with little relation to what has gone before. This provides a sensible context for understanding Kerr and Stattin's conclusion: "It would be a mistake to conclude, however, that child disclosure is something completely separate from anything parents do, because parents' actions probably play a role in a child's willingness to disclose. How parents have reacted to information in the past and how accepting and warm they are, in general, are likely to influence disclosure. . . . Parents' past solicitation efforts could influence child disclosure by encouraging the child to develop a habit of disclosing. Very young children could begin talking to parents about their daily activities because the parents ask and listen with interest and this could become habitual until the disclosure is independent of parents' asking" (p. 378). As always, an ounce of prevention is worth a pound of cure.

Another complicating element is that the typical teenage brain is still in many ways more like the brain of a child. As documented by Shannon Brownlee writing in *U.S. News & World Report* in August 1999, when it comes to brain development, " . . . one of the last parts to mature is in charge of making sound judgment and calming unruly emotions, and the emotional centers in the teenage brain have already been revving up, probably under the influence of sex hormones" (p. 47). Thus, one source of the secret lives of teenagers is that they themselves sometimes are "in the dark" about what they are doing and why. As a result, they misinterpret behavior, even their own, and may mislabel the nature of their conduct.

We must add the fact that brain researchers have found that teenagers are often not very effective in identifying the emotional significance of facial expressions (for example, about two thirds missed the emotion of fear in a series of pictures and mislabeled it anger or discomfort, while none of the adults studied did so). This confusion, too, can contribute to the teenagers having a hard time reporting to parents.

Secrecy on the Dark Side

Some kids have more than normal secrets. Some kids develop a dark, distorted inner life. Parents often find out about this only after some catastrophe has happened. For example, Dylan Klebold's parents were stunned to find out how distorted his thinking and feeling had become in the months prior to his assault on Columbine High School. The videotapes he and his co-conspirator Eric Harris made were a shocking revelation for the parents. As reported in *Time* magazine, Eric and Dylan appear on tape saying things like this:

Dylan Klebold says: "I'm sorry I have so much rage," and tells his parents they've "been great parents" who taught him "self-awareness, self-reliance . . . I always appreciated that." And, the morning of the shooting, "It's a half-hour before our Judgment Day. I didn't like life very much. Just know I'm going to a better place than here." And, "It's what we had to do." Addressing his tormentors, "I'm going to kill you all. You've been driving us s—for years."

Eric Harris says: "It f—ing sucks to do this to them. They're going to be put through hell." And, "I wish they were out of town so I didn't have to look at them and bond more." And, "I know my mom and dad will be in shock and disbelief. I can't help it." He says, "It's what we had to do. I'm sorry. Like Shakespeare says, 'Good wombs hath born bad sons.'"

In a lecture to a meeting of psychotherapists in April 2000, Jim was presenting an analysis of the dynamics of secret lives among disturbed teenagers. During the question-and-answer period a therapist rose and said, "I can't believe that this is possible in a good family. My definition of a good family is one in which there is good communication between parents and kids (and between parents). Therefore, I think the parents must have had a bad relationship with their son for this to happen, for him to have such a secret life."

In response, a psychiatrist named Diane Schetky stood and responded thus: "I was asked to interview Michael Carneal, the school shooter in West Paducah, Kentucky. He was so paranoid and distrustful that it makes perfect sense to me that he worked hard to keep his parents in the dark about what was going on inside him." This boy had a secret list of insults in his head that dated back to elementary school. No one knew the extent to which he harbored grudges and had developed a secret inner world from which the assault on his school arose.

Kip Kinkel, the 15-year-old boy who killed his parents prior to attacking his school—and killing two students—reported during his interrogation and confession that he had been hearing voices. Others among the school shooters who received so much media attention in recent years have made similar disclosures. One common theme is that they tried to hide their growing disturbance from their parents.

Why Can't Parents Discover the Secret Life?

Why can't parents discover the secret life of their teenager? Like all the tough questions, this one has many answers. For one thing, most parents have a concept of who their child is, and it is difficult to receive information that contradicts that concept. In a sense, it seems disloyal to be *capable* of thinking the worst of your child. Parental love is strong—and sometimes blind.

Second, parents don't have all the information about their children. This is in part because they have no connection with people outside the family who know their child. Sometimes it is because others deliberately withhold information about the child. Sometimes it is because the behavior of children and teenagers differs from setting to setting.

Most of us think kids have one identity, but actually they may have several. Social psychologists call this the *fundamental attribution error*—the tendency to focus on one set of character traits in a person based upon seeing them in one situation and then neglecting to see who the person is in other settings and contexts. At the "normal" end of the continuum, many kids have somewhat different personalities at home and at school, for example. The same shy, polite child at home may be boisterous and loud at school. At the "abnormal" end of this continuum, some kids actually are different people in the two settings. This is often the case with kids who are so deeply troubled that they are en route to being psychopaths, the proverbial "nice guy" who turns out to be a mass murderer.

And, of course, some kids deliberately set out to deceive their parents. They create secret lives at home—and perhaps even with other adults, such as teachers—in order to screen their secret lives on the dark side of the culture. Writing in *Time* magazine in May 1999, columnist Amy Dickenson put it this way: "Teenagers are good at hiding their true selves—or the selves they're trying out this month—behind the "grandma face" they wear when they're trotted out to see the relatives. Behind that pleasant mask there can be volumes of bad poetry, body piercing, and tattoos" (p. 40). But this, too, is not confined to children and youth. Adults sometimes have dark secret lives that they fiercely work to keep private for fear that disclosure will open them to ridicule or legal sanctions.

How It Looks Depends Upon Where You Stand

Yet another issue in understanding the secret lives of teenagers is the way kids and their parents differ in their interpretation of family events and history. The documentary about Kip Kinkel (the school shooter in Springfield, Oregon) is painful to watch for many reasons. One is the discrepancy between the way he saw his family life and the way his parents did. Kip's parents were good people, highly motivated to raise their two children according to high standards. They were loving and kind, and skilled in dealing with children (both were successful teachers).

Nonetheless, it seems Kip experienced his family as something quite different. He experienced being the black sheep of the family, the inadequate son whose competence paled before that of his successful sister. He felt troubled and angry about his inferior position and character within the family. Seeing the family videos, we can imagine how he learned this.

But could his parents see it? We doubt it. In all likelihood, what they saw was a troubled boy, who seemed to defeat all their best efforts to teach and help him. They saw themselves as being fair and loving both their children. They looked at the success of their daughter and wondered why their son could not be more like her.

Tough as it is for us as parents to see the world through the eyes of our children, we must. Here's what one teenage girl wrote about the treatment she and her brother received at home from her loving and caring parents.

My being born was a big blow to my older brother's ego. He started stuttering while our mom was pregnant with me. He was only six, and had been used to being an only child, liked and had been so for six years. I think he eventually got used to me, tolerated my presence, assuming that if he bided his time, that he could get rid of me. He would often try to sell me to strangers, even give me away, seemingly very comical and innocent to the adults whom he involved in his transactions, but deadly serious to him. And I adored him.

As we got older, the differences between me and my brother grew even more apparent. I always used to think that my mom liked my brother more and that he was more like her. They were both a little touchy, excitable. I was more like my dad, laid back and taking everything in stride. The difference was, and I see it even more now that I'm older, that my mom tried her hardest to shower her affection on us equally. I was the proverbial Daddy's little girl, and I think my brother saw this and it hurt him.

Years have intensified the rift between my brother and my dad. Neither one agrees with the way the other lives his life, and stuck in the middle is me, loving both, not totally agreeing with either. I think it hurts my brother to see how different our father treats us . . . and though the reasons for this are numerous and valid, my brother sees it as a direct attack on his status in the family.

When the father in question read this, he responded,

I was astounded by my daughter's analysis of my relationship with her brother. I acknowledge that I have always thought she was more like me, as she points out. But what I find amazing is that she doesn't see the intensity of my bond with her brother, my deep love for him. As a baby and a toddler, I spent much more time with him than I ever did with her. I took him with me on professional trips whenever I could. He and I were inseparable. But he was a much more temperamentally challenging child than she. This meant I had to do much more for him when it came to teaching him to deal with his temperamental vulnerabilities and helping him develop the kind of character and coping strategies that would protect and strengthen him. But in my heart of hearts, when I am calm and not defensive, I can see how all these efforts in the years after she was born would look like favoritism to her (and I guess to her brother). It may be years before these two kids sort things out in their relationships with me—I know it took me a long time to see my own childhood and parents clearly.

When the System Perpetuates the Secret Lives of Kids

At times, the very systems that have a significant influence in our children's lives contribute, at times unknowingly, to the problem of secrets in the lives of our children. Here is a case in point, the story of Nancy, the mother of 12-year-old Tyrone.

There are parents who would say I'm a hysterical mother and I am blowing this out of proportion. The parents of this child are saying exactly that . . . But the principal of my son's middle school says that he has seen a lot of things, but that this feels creepy to him. My 12-year-old son is my last child. I have put three other kids through school—I have two older kids who are in their twenties now and whom I have put through high school. I have experience with the school system. Therefore, I don't think I am overreacting. Nothing like this has ever happened to my other children. Nothing this direct, or with this level of violence. I always preface my comments to the superintendent saying that I've put kids through the school system before, and this is not about the typical mother of a baby boomer who is overly protective. They assure me that they don't think I am being overreactive and that they are taking this seriously.

It started a year ago. We heard about it only last fall. Apparently, there had been trouble with this kid against my kid—my son is twelve and in seventh grade. When he was in sixth grade, apparently incidents had been happening and we never heard about it. It was September or October, I got a voice mail at work saying, "Tyrone is being stalked, I am on the way to the school right now to speak to the principal." That is the first time I had heard anything about it, and I hear this on my voice mail! I call the office, I call home, there is no answer. What we ended up learning is that my older son, who is a freshman in high school, came home on that day, it was a Friday, and said, "Do you know that Tyrone is being stalked?" He said that a kid came up to him at school and told him, "Are you Tyrone's brother? Do you know that he is being stalked?" This is a kid at my older son's high school, and *he* is aware that my youngest son is being stalked at the middle school. I don't know how he found this out, but he informed my older son that there was a mediation process already going at the middle school, related to this stalking issue about which we had heard nothing until that Friday! My older son came home and immediately told my husband, and that is when my husband called the school and said he would be over there now. What had turned out is that earlier that week, this kid had done something which we found out he had been doing for the whole previous year: he follows Tyrone around in the hallways, he stares him down—that is, he'll just stand there and watch him intensely until he gets to where he is supposed to be, he "fake" punches him, that is, he'll kick his foot as he walks by to try to hit him. In gym class, he'd go up to him and say "I'm going to get you" and then leave. Apparently, the hallway incident had happened earlier that week, and a kid in the hall said to Tyrone, "Why don't you file a harassment complaint?" We're talking about eleven- or twelve-year-olds . . . But apparently, there is such a procedure in the middle school, and Tyrone filed a complaint. It's different from when I grew up, that's for sure! I mean I would have never thought of filing a harassment complaint . . . But then when *I* was growing up, the worst problem

I had was someone calling me names . . . I know people tend to idealize the past, but it does seem that kids today encounter the kinds of situations we never even thought of. To go back to Tyrone's story, the situation resulted in the local mediation service coming in and doing a mediation between this kid and my son. My husband and I were all over the assistant vice principal about the fact that a mediation had been going on—we told her, "How could a mediation be going on with community dispute resolution and you never called the parents to tell them this was happening? This is a twelve-year-old kid. Is this not something you would call the parents about? You call about a kid showing up late for class, but not for this?" Her answer to us was "Typical school procedure. Didn't think that there was anything wrong with not notifying the parents." She even tried to throw it back onto us. "Why didn't your kid tell you that this is what was happening?" she said. I since have asked my son all about it, of course, but he never brought it up on his own! My point is that the school has a responsibility to keep parents informed, and in this case, they did not. The school's attitude was to keep the problem "within the school." But if they take it to outside mediation, it is an indication that the situation is serious enough, and then the school should be more concerned about involving the parents than about keeping things under a lid.

Through the mediation office, whose director my husband and I happened to know, we found out that it had been a failed mediation process. The kid would not indicate why he was doing what he was doing to my son; he became very emotional and was not able to participate in the mediation. Again through the mediator, we learned for the first time about the extent of the harassment behavior and the threats against Tyrone. Most critically, we found out that this kid was keeping a log of my son's activities. He has a daily log about what Tyrone wears, who he talks to, where he lives. I've seen pages of the log, and there are entries about where I work, what color my house is, the tree behind it . . . keeping a computer log of my son and his family. That is unsettling. There was even a rumor that this kid has produced a Web page titled Ten Ways to Kill Tyrone M. That Web page was talked about by several school kids. After this failed attempt at mediation, the kid was given a one-day school suspension, and Tyrone was told that he was to report any interaction with this kid. Within that first week, he was given a page from the computer log—another schoolmate had borrowed a disk from this kid, opened the disk and found the log about Tyrone's activities, printed it and brought it to him, saying, "You need to know about what this kid is doing." The log recorded "Tyrone M. wore his blue and yellow shirt outside his pants today, different than the way he wore it last week." It was creepy. Just absolutely creepy. He's listing where my husband works, in addition to where I work. Tyrone brought the log to the school administration. At that point, the administration seemed to be paying a little more attention. Now that they had proof of the log. This was within two weeks of my husband and me finding out what had been going on for over a year. I began to seriously worry about what else this kid might have on my son, what else was going on. The school asked if I would be uncomfortable talking with the parents of the kid, and a meeting was arranged.

When we arrived for the meeting, we were told the father was away on a business trip but had sent a fax to the school saying we were all blowing this out of proportion, and he did not want this meeting to occur. The mother arrived and, despite her husband's fax, agreed to speak with us. She seemed fairly open, but the kind of information she shared reminded me of the kinds of things we heard about Eric Harris or Dylan Klebold: he has a real hard time in social situations, he has a real hard time making friends, he seems to be more of a social outcast and we are aware of that. I was going away on a business trip and he asked me to get him a book on how to make friends. Her understanding of the problem between our sons is that there was a friend of her son's who now was a friend of Tyrone's, and no longer a friend of her son's, and so her son was jealous that my son had taken his friend away. She felt that was what precipitated this kind of behavior in her son. That it was the "motive." But in reality this "stolen" friend was really only an acquaintance to Tyrone, not a buddy. This was not just about one kid being angry at another for taking a friend. It was distorted thinking on the kid's part. The fact that her son was keeping a computerized log on my child for the last year could not be taken lightly, in my view. Her response to this was that she considers her son's computer his personal diary and would not invade his right to privacy. She considered the stalking journal his "personal diary." I felt my child's safety was more important than her son's right to his computer privacy. Something is wrong with that.

The principal's office persisted in trying to keep a lid on things, saying "Let's make sure we are all talking to each other, and let's just be aware of the situation, and we'll make sure that we watch things." Very nonchalant, in my view. We told the school we would go to the police, and they again assured us that there was no need to take this out of the school.

Conclusion

When something goes wrong with kids, many people are ready to blame the parents. And yet, research shows that many kids have secret lives—dangerous, illegal, and/or disturbing experiences, feelings, and thoughts, about which their parents know nothing. Sometimes this is due to parental neglect, but mostly it is due to the deliberate and often clever steps kids take to keep their secret lives secret. What's a parent to do? How can parents identify dangerous signals in their kids?

There is a difference between parents who actively contribute to the unhealthy development of their children and those who fail despite their best efforts. If we are to learn anything from the horrible experience of the Klebolds in Colorado, and the other parents who have lost children to the secrets of the dark side, it is that none of us should be smug and complacent. It is literally a matter of "there but for the grace of God go I." Some children make it through childhood seemingly intact, but have accumulated risks in the way they look at the world, the way they feel about the world, and the way they understand their role in the world. When these vulnerable children enter adolescence and confront the nastiness and the bullying and the social toxicity, they may begin to lose their way.

When these kids become so troubled in their thinking and their feeling that they lose touch with normal reality, with its ups and downs, they are in extreme danger. Some of these kids present special challenges to parents by virtue of the fact that they may have serious mental disturbances, such as depression. Peer influences unknown to the parent may compound and feed these problems, as may the toxic culture of adolescence.

In less socially complicated times, emotional and physical closeness to their children may indeed have earned parents an accurate understanding of what was going on in their kids' lives, and secrets may well have been less severe in their potential consequences. But even without indulging in a sense of nostalgia for simpler times, most of us who are parents admit that it is difficult to relate to the dangers looming in our children's lives today, compared to what we faced growing up. Life does seem more complicated for parents as well as for growing children, and the buffers against dangers do seem to have been shrinking rather than increasing.

Lesson: You can be in the same room with your child and yet not be present; the doorway to the secret life of kids opens only to parents who can listen without judgment and who receive the information they need to understand the inner life of their child, from the child and from other sources in their child's world, such as peers, school, and the community. However, some children create such an impermeable secret life that they succeed in keeping their parents unaware of that part of their lives.

Part Two

A Parent's Compass

6

Using Intelligent Empathy to Raise a Child with a Difficult Temperament

Understanding the Child's Mysteries

A child can be an open book one minute and a mystery the next. But challenging children may seem more mysterious than most much of the time. A child plays with dolls in bizarre ways, or will not move a toy out of its special corner, or insists he is a helicopter. A little girl screams when another child touches her toy; a baby boy fusses and protests when his mother tries to hold him close. Loving, nonviolent parents are baffled and frustrated by their child's aggression. How can we face these mysteries successfully? To do so, we must develop in ourselves the greatest possible creative intuition and insight. With insight we are capable of meeting the challenge posed by the difficult child. What it takes is a mix of insightful analysis of a child's behavior and the ability to feel and see things as they see and feel them. We call this double ability *intelligent empathy.*

Consider David, a 5-year-old boy observed in the school yard eating a banana. When the boy finished his healthy snack, he dropped the peel on the ground. The principal saw this, came over, and told him to pick it up. The boy picked it up and put it back down. The principal said, "Pick it up and put it in the trash." The boy picked it up and put it in the trash can. After waiting a minute, he picked it out again and put it on the ground. Then the principal ordered him to pick it up, put it in the trash, and leave it there. The child did so, then stood there a moment longer, picked up the peel again and once more put it on the ground until the principal finally said in exasperation, "Pick up the peel. Put it in the trash, and leave it there forever!"

This was a bright, but troubled, child. As a young teacher, Jim set about the task of trying to form a relationship with him but seemed to make little headway until one day in the art room, when he sat across from David as the little boy began to draw. Inspiration struck, and Jim began to copy David's drawing. Eventually, the little boy realized what Jim was doing, but made no comment. When he finished the first drawing, he began a second. Jim copied that one too. Upon finishing the second drawing, David smiled his impish smile and said, "Now you draw one." Jim did, and David began to copy. The result? Jim became David's buddy, and this experience formed the basis for a relationship that eventually translated into other friendships in the school. Little David was on the road to integration into the school community in a way that had seemed impossible previously.

Why did this work? To a degree, it is a mystery. But we suspect that this little boy was responding to Jim's playful approach, which in turn gave David a chance to lead, something that happened rarely in his controlled life at home. Adult and child were playing, and that was the start of something important. In play, children take control by playing different roles, by moving from passivity to activity. Challenging children need help with this process, in learning it, and in feeling confident enough to take it on. For adults to know how and when to intervene in this playful manner requires insight.

Adults need to develop at least two kinds of creative insight in their relationships with children. The first, and most common, is when someone knows what is going on inside a particular child because of a special relationship with *that* child. Psychologist Urie Bronfenbrenner often said that the key to good child development is the child having at least one adult who is crazy about that child, someone who believes the sun rises and sets on that child. This commitment is intensely individualized. This is the kind of insight parents develop most of the time from living with their child. Mom says, "Something's going on with Bob today. I just know something's wrong." And Dad replies, "I noticed it too. Maybe something happened at school today." Parents know a child in depth, in detail, and in context. That knowledge is specific to a particular child and may not generalize to all children.

The second kind of insight is more general. It is the ability to understand *children*, being able to understand a child even without having a long-standing special relationship with that child. This is what teachers and other professionals count on in their work and parents rely upon with other people's children. A 6-year-old plays with puppets as his therapist watches the melodrama that unfolds between the big bear and the little bear. The therapist says to the child, "I think you are angry at your dad because you think he is going to leave you the way he left your mom." She says this in light of what she has just seen. But she also knows about children, and she has practiced listening to children.

This second kind of insightful ability takes hard work, study, and emotional commitment on the part of the adult. It results from firmly believing that what children do and say makes sense if approached from the child's point of view. And it comes from looking anew, with this new insight, into the meaning of what children do and say right before us—at the dinner table, in the car, on the playground, getting ready for bed.

Psychoanalyst Bruno Bettelheim and psychiatrist Alvin Rosenfeld called this "the art of the obvious." It takes a willingness to use your own experience as a way to make contact. It takes a commitment to put judgment aside in favor of acceptance, substitute knowledge of child development for bias and myth, and be willing to open oneself to the child's emotions rather than experiencing everything from an adult viewpoint. When all of this is put together, we call it intelligent empathy. Sometimes even children can do it.

In *The Boy Who Would Be a Helicopter,* early childhood educator Vivian Paley's book describes her experience with a young child who entered her class one September unwilling to relate to other children or adults except within his self-proclaimed identity as a helicopter. The little boy carried a toy helicopter with him always and refused invitations to join in any other form of play. The wonderful educational environment of Paley's class was not accessible to him because he was held captive by internal forces, forces of fear that led him to the conclusion that the world was too dangerous a place to experience as a child.

What had happened to this innocent little boy that he had withdrawn from the reality of his identity as being a child, not a machine? Paley learned that his family's apartment had been broken into repeatedly over the preceding years, and the situation reached such a crisis that the family abruptly moved to a new apartment across the street from a hospital. The little boy's window faced out on the hospital's helicopter landing pad. Presumably, the helicopter became a vivid symbol of his new safety. Whatever the exact reason, the boy was both reassured and trapped by his identification with the helicopter. Paley tried to free him, but her efforts were to no avail.

Finally, the boy was reconnected through the intervention of a child in Paley's class. The little girl approached her young classmate with the proposition "Let's play helicopter family, and you can be the baby helicopter and I will be the mommy helicopter." The boy accepted this offer to play on these terms, and it was the beginning of his liberation. Eventually, he was able to connect with other children and his teacher. Once the bridge had been built, he was able to start along the road to freedom. His timid temperament coupled with his traumatic experience had set him on the road to trouble; an insightful intervention had turned him around.

A challenging child was transformed. It all starts with understanding children, and understanding temperament. Temperament sets the terms of relationship and interaction between children and adults, but it need not control that interaction and relationship if the parents have insight, of both the specific and the general kind.

Another Look at Temperament

In Chapter 3 we wrestled with the issue of how impossible a difficult child can become. By peering through the microscope of our ecological perspective, we see the roots of impossibility in a combination of child temperament and experience, in the family and the larger community—school, neighborhood, and society. Sometimes parents create an impossible child who is not predisposed to it temperamentally. They do this through ambivalent or negligent parenting, turning an ordinary baby into a challenging toddler, and perhaps even a delinquent or antisocial teenager. We saw that process at work in Chapter 3. But how do we save temperamentally vulnerable and challenging infants from becoming the impossible children in the first place?

First we must understand more fully the process through which temperament can evolve into someone's personality. Like all psychological terms, temperament has a simple definition and a complex one. The simple definition will suffice for us, and it goes like this: Children enter the world with different packages of physical, emotional and physiological attributes that affect how they feel inside themselves, how they perceive the world, how they respond to the world and find their place in that world.

Some infants are so highly sensitive in one or more of their senses that the world seems louder, brighter, or smellier than it does to other babies. Some shrink back from what they sense; others reach out to look, listen, taste, and touch. Some feel comfortable in their bodies (and others are uneasy in their own skin). In *Temperament Talk: A Guide to Understanding Your Child,* an excellent handbook for parents, Kathy Goodman, Lyndall Shick, Barbara Tyler, and Barbara Zukin define temperament in parent-friendly language as "the set of traits each of us is born with. It is our own unique style, the starting point for personality. It is what makes some things easy for us, and other things hard."

No kid is exactly like another. One 17-year-old girl described herself as a Mercedes Benz in comparison with her brother. "I just needed an oil change every three thousand miles to keep me purring along," she said. "I was an easy baby right from the start. My brother, on the other hand, was like a sports car my parents once had—exciting but prone to break down."

Some children are physically insensitive in the sense that it takes a lot more physical stimulation to get a reaction. These children may seek out rough-and-tumble play or extreme sports that a more sensitive child would shun as overwhelming. In teenagers, the physical systems that underlie temperament may be painfully evident in the way they describe what it is like to be them, as it coalesces into a negative view of self. Sixteen-year-old Steve put it this way: "Sometimes I just hate the way I feel. I get cranky and out of sorts and I feel mad and my whole body drives me crazy. Then I take it out on my girlfriend or my mom. It's just the way I am. I can't help it." As we shall see, however, the good news for Steve—and everyone else in his life—is that it *can* be helped.

The good news is that parents can learn how to cope with temperamentally difficult children. Ross Greene's book *The Explosive Child* gives parents a lot of helpful advice on this score. He offers parents a clear understanding of how and why some children are prone to "meltdown," along with some strategies for coping with the "impossible" demands of the explosive child. He encourages parents to acknowledge the fact that for some of these children—particularly if they have not been managed effectively in early childhood—it may be necessary to arrange out-of-home placement, what he describes in a chapter entitled "Change of Venue." He describes in detail how excruciatingly emotional and financially costly the change of venue option is for families. But he makes clear how and when this option is the most loving, caring option in a difficult situation with no easy and cheap alternatives.

For families facing such a tough decision, the help of a professional educational consultant can prove an excellent investment (and the Web site listed in the resource section at the end of this book may be helpful in identifying such a consultant). A knowledgeable professional can help parents match their child's special needs to a setting that can help meet those needs, and help parents deal with the guilt and feelings of defeat they may feel at sending their child away. Evidence of the effectiveness of residential programs like "therapeutic wilderness programs" is encouraging. The combination of physical challenge, exposure to nature, and therapy does make a difference in the out-of-control behavior of many difficult kids.

We recognize that part of the problem we all face is cultural, because as Americans we have a prejudice against residential programs for kids. We are afraid of them, and we are inclined to stigmatize them. Other societies—as in Israel, for example—have a different approach. It is much more common in other societies for kids, particularly teenagers, to live apart from their families. This normalizing of out-of-home living for teenagers provides a more supportive cultural climate for the parent facing a difficult child who needs a change of venue. But even in America there are options that parents must consider when all the in-home alternatives have been explored and tried out without success.

Greene offers compelling examples like Jennifer, who when little was clearly impossible as a result of her explosive temperament. Although her parents tried to adapt, they did not have the knowledge or skills needed to succeed early. By fifth grade her troubles at home were becoming more and more evident at school—skipping classes, complaining, being disobedient and defiant. Her parents and siblings had been involved in a long series of therapists, medications, and confrontations. As the mother reports, "She's been like that since she was born." Finally, as the danger to Jennifer and her family reaches a critical point, Greene offers the following: "We've been at this for quite a while now. . . . I'm afraid it's becoming obvious that we are not going to achieve our goals through outpatient treatment. I think we should consider looking for a place outside your home." It can reach that point.

But just coming to the realization that home is not enough for some children isn't the end of the process. For many families it is only the beginning of a long, frustrating, and painful process, a process that is so important that if it fails the results can be catastrophic. Lisa's story of her family's struggle is a cautionary tale for any of us.

We decided we would take Philip out of the high school and place him in a therapeutic program and then a private school. We started by looking for an educational consultant and found one, but we couldn't afford him. Then we did our own research into programs, and found out that the good ones cost anywhere from $18,000 to $30,000. We just did not have that kind of money, no matter how much we wished we did. So my husband and I took matters into our own hands. We finally found one that had a place for him and that our insurance would cover. We drove one thousand miles to get him there, taking turns between the two of us to sit next to Philip so he would not jump out of the van. He stayed at the program a few weeks, then he left. He was sixteen years old. He hitchhiked all the way back to our town. Apparently, some woman took pity on him and housed him for three days until one of his buddies could pick him up. He stayed home briefly, and during that time we found a school out of state that seemed right for his special needs. We thought this would be a great step forward, and made all the arrangements for him to begin his senior year there. The day before we were to drive him there, the school informed us there had been a mistake and that Philip was on a waiting list. His name never did make it to the top of the list, and he did not get in. That was a huge disappointment and humiliation for him, and from then on, he seemed to give up. He returned to his regular school in the fall, but hardly ever attended classes. His behavior continued to deteriorate, and by then, we were becoming exhausted and depleted, unsure about what to do next. Two weeks ago, Philip moved out. I heard from him yesterday for the first time since he left. He was calling from a public phone. He said he's living on the street, sleeping on park benches, and that he wants it this way for now.

We believe parents who are dealing with such very difficult and seemingly hopeless situations can draw some strength from the wisdom of great spiritual teachers. When everything seems to be falling apart, it becomes imperative that parents find inspiration so as not to lose all hope, whatever their spiritual faith. Here is a letter that one mother wrote to her son after sending him to a therapeutic boarding school. Her son struggles with issues of addiction and depression, and was failing school.

Dear Derrick:

I was looking through the Dalai Lama's Web site and found a page on some questions that were asked him, along with his answers. I think a lot about your drug issues and your anger, and all that, and I ask myself, What would it take for Derrick to move away from the darkness in his life and into the light? I want only your *true* happiness. Not happiness based on temporary happy moments that only lead to pain afterwards.

In Buddhism, the main emphasis is on looking into one's own mind. Nobody can do it for us. We can go to therapy, which is helpful, but if we don't do something to learn how to be in charge of our minds and of our emotions, therapy efforts don't last very long. What follows is the Dalai Lama's answer to feeling depressed. If you read and reread the first paragraph, and really try to understand what it says, you will be closer to finding what it takes to be truly happy. I believe that our anger and pain is in part something we brought into this life from past lifetimes, and it is something for us to work through in this life. There is no escaping our minds and the past habits we have brought back with us into this lifetime. There is only working through it. Drugs help you forget the pain temporarily, but the pain will always come back if you don't work through your issues by taming your own mind yourself. Drugs won't be there when you leave this life, and sooner or later, you will have to begin the work of regaining charge over your thoughts. That's my wish for you. True happiness and healing your thoughts so your emotions can heal too.

Q&A to the Dalai Lama:

Q: If we have committed a serious negative act, how can we let go of the feeling of guilt that may follow?

A: In such situations, where there is a danger of feeling guilty and therefore depressed, the Buddhist point of view advises adopting certain ways of thinking and behaving which will enable you to recover your self-confidence. A Buddhist may reflect on the nature of his mind, i.e., on its essential purity, and in what way disturbing thoughts and their subsequent emotions are of an entirely different nature. Because such disturbing emotions are adventitious, they can be eliminated. To think of the immense well of potential hidden deep within our being, to understand that the nature of the mind is fundamental purity and kindness, and to meditate on its luminosity will enable you to develop self-confidence and courage.

The Buddha says in the Sutras that fully enlightened and omniscient beings, whom we consider to be superior, did not spring from the bowels of the earth, nor did they fall from the sky; they are the result of spiritual purification. Such beings were once as troubled as we are now, with the same weaknesses and flaws of ordinary beings. Shakyamuni Buddha himself, prior to his enlightenment, lived in other incarnations that were far more difficult than our present lives. To recognize, in all its majesty, our own potential for spiritual perfection is an antidote to guilt, disgust, and hopelessness. Nagarjuna says in *The Precious Garland of Advice for the King* that pessimism and depression never help in finding a good solution to any problem. On the other hand, arrogance is just as negative. But to present as an antidote to it a posture of extreme humility may tend to foster a lack of self-confidence and open the door to depression and discouragement. We would only go from one extreme to the other.

I would like to point out that to set out on a retreat for three years full of hope and expectations, thinking that without the slightest difficulty you will come out of it fully enlightened, can turn into a disaster unless you undertake it with the most serious intentions. If you overestimate your expectations and have too much self-confidence, you will be headed for dissatisfaction and disillusionment. When you think of what the Buddha said—that perfect enlightenment is the result of spiritual purification and an accumulation of virtues and wisdom for eons and eons—it is certain that courage and perseverance will arise to accompany you on the path.

This particular mother leans on Buddhist teachings as her life jacket, but this is only one source of practical spiritual wisdom among a larger pool of different spiritual views. Whatever the particular emphasis of one's beliefs, each of us can find inspiration and direction in some spiritual teaching, no matter what tradition is most in line with who we are. The point is to be sure that we do not ignore or take for granted this wisdom in our efforts to love difficult children and prevent their further slide into the dark side of human experience.

Who Are These Challenging Children?

Parental horror stories about placing difficult children are all too common. But in most cases, where effective understanding and intervention starts early it need not come to that. As National Institute of Mental Health psychiatrist Stanley Greenspan shows us in his book *The Challenging Child*, parents can actually help their children make the most of their temperament, whatever it is. They can do this by turning challenge into opportunity, especially if they start early enough.

Who are these challenging children? Greenspan draws from the best child development research to group children into five major temperamental patterns. Greenspan is a great advocate for children and parents. Thus, he recognizes that each type of child has strengths. He encourages parents to play to these strengths while compensating for the child's temperamental vulnerabilities. He has seen how even the most challenging child can turn out well. Greenspan provides all the details. Here we will simply provide an outline of his approach.

• *Highly Sensitive*

These children feel everything more intensely than most. There are physiological reasons for this, as Carol Kranowitz points out in her book *The Out-of-Sync Child*. The world to them is full of extreme sensations—like being at a rock concert all the time. At each stage along the developmental way, these children find the world so intense, they react with a mixture of outrage and withdrawal. As babies, they cry a great deal and are irritable and demanding. As preschoolers they resist change and are fearful. As school-age children they are self-centered and grandiose in their fears and demands. If handled well, however, these children can become creative and insightful, and use their sensitivity as the basis for empathy and compassion. Success comes from a combination of empathy, structure and clearly established limits, encouragement of initiative, and self-observation.

• *Self-absorbed*

In contrast to highly sensitive children, self-absorbed children often seem "easy" at the start. They make few demands and seem content to be left alone with their own inner world. As babies they sleep a great deal and don't cry much. As they move through the first year, however, this easiness becomes less appealing because the child does not respond well to the social overtures of parents—smiling, talking, playing peek-aboo—that are one of the main ways parents get reinforced for the efforts they invest in child rearing.

The core problem is that human development is fundamentally a social process, and self-absorbed children are not very social. They stay on the periphery at the playground and at school. Their inner lives seem more real to them than the world around them. There is a danger that parents will give up on such children. Success comes from parental leadership, or as Greenspan puts it, "energetic wooing in order to be pulled into the world." These children are often slow to warm, and it takes more time and energy on the part of adults to get them going in the right developmental direction. The terms of engagement change as the child matures—from floor play with infants and toddlers to playground games with elementary school children to interactive board games as they get older. The goal at each point is the same: to engage the child and build social momentum.

• *Defiant*

Greenspan says it well: "Stubborn, negative, controlling— the defiant child manages to turn even the simplest activity into a trial." Like highly sensitive children, defiant children find the world an intense experience. But unlike highly sensitive children, defiant children do not shrink from that world and whine; they seek to dominate and control it—and that includes their parents. While it is normal for children to explore the word "no" as a tool for defining who they are and how the world works, defiant children get stuck on "no."

Transitions are often a focal point for defiance, from the everyday transitions of getting up in the morning to getting ready for bed at night. But the larger life transitions are involved in this negativism as well, from toilet training and starting school to taking on chores and meeting curfews. This negativism is usually coupled with a high level of energy and persistence, so many parents have to deal not with "no," but with "no, no, no, no, no, no, no, no. . . ." Add to this cleverness (to defeat parental arguments), deceptiveness (to get around your rules), and stubbornness, and it is a long, exhausting road for the parents of a defiant child.

But it is a road that can also lead to good things. It requires extraordinary patience and self-control on the part of parents. The key is "persuade, negotiate, and set limits in a calm, empathic, and supportive way." Defiant children don't back down much; they only dig their heels in deeper in the face of efforts to intimidate them. The goal for parents and other adults is to work together to see the underlying insecurities and vulnerabilities of these children and be as soothing as possible while at the same time setting limits on their behavior. Underneath the rude and obnoxious behavior may lie a highly sensitive child who is defending him- or herself against being overwhelmed. That is why self-awareness is so important for both parents and children.

Older defiant children can be helped to be aware of their sensitivities and tolerance level. This awareness allows the talents of defiant children to flow into pro-social paths; these children can become very successful adults, particularly in fields in which persistence and organization are an asset. This means parents and teachers must spend a lot of time helping the child with words and ideas to capture their experience and bring it to consciousness—"You are feeling mad right now, aren't you?" the parent says to the 4-year-old who is launching into a tirade of "no." "Tell me in words what you are angry about."

• *Inattentive*

While the issue of "attention deficit" has become a common theme in the way parents and teachers view children, Greenspan is critical of simplistic thinking about this issue, particularly when they are diagnosed too readily as having Attention Deficit Disorder (ADD). He says, "In some cases, children believed to suffer from ADD are being medicated without adequate medical, developmental, and mental health evaluations to determine whether they actually have an attention difficulty or some other challenges and whether medication is needed."

He offers parents a more sophisticated view of this issue by pointing out that the best research shows that paying attention is composed of many specific mental processes and that these processes work in specific contexts, not across the board. This is crucial to understanding inattentive children and to knowing how to help them proceed developmentally. For most children, it is the details of school life that are the biggest problem—writing, repetitive arithmetic problems, and other features of the "boring" routine of day-to-day life in most schools.

When it comes to sitting down one-on-one in a quiet setting and talking about things of interest to the child, the picture is usually very different. The same "attention deficits" often disappear, and what emerges is an interesting child! How can parents and other adults help these children proceed? In Greenspan's view, the key is training these children to be self-observant, to work on their skills, to articulate how they experience paying attention to specific tasks. For example, the teacher or parent can help the child make decisions and limit choices. Instead of going to the ice cream store and asking, "What do you want?" the parent should plan out a set of limited choices. Thus, on the way to the store the parent might say, "You can choose from these three flavors." This prevents the child from being overwhelmed by the thirty-six flavors available once they get to the store. Of course, the effectiveness of this approach hinges upon the parent knowing the child well enough to choose three good flavors.

This self-awareness can help the children and the adults who care for them organize activities to work better. How? One way is to find the topics or activities that are most pleasurable, and therefore in which persistence and paying attention operate well for the child. Knowing this, adults can devise strategies to accomplish the important learning goals through other activities that parallel these intrinsically well-matched activities. This harnesses their positive emotional energy in the service of learning and development. It is truly a positive, asset-focused approach to parenting and educating these children.

• *Active/Aggressive*

Interestingly, Greenspan links together "active" and "aggressive," and he takes a different tack than many temperament researchers do. But his link offers an important clue to the larger question of rearing such children successfully. Children are not born aggressive; they learn to be aggressive. But children are born active and impulsive, and unless the activity and impulsivity are handled correctly, they can serve as the foundation for building aggression. The long-term payoff of high or hyper activity levels gone positive is seen in the careers of athletes, soldiers, and many of society's movers and shakers. On the other hand, the long-term costs of this same hyper level of physical activity channeled in destructive ways can be seen in prisons.

The stakes are high, and the challenge to parents equally so. Greenspan writes,

> There is probably no greater challenge for a parent than coping with an angry child. If the active/aggressive child's temperament is allowed to control parental response, the long pattern is likely to be one of accentuating the inherent challenges into a spiraling pattern of difficulty. But if the parents understand the cause-effect chains that arise when activity/aggression controls their interaction with the child, they can de-escalate and re-channel and calm the child. At

the extremes, when these children face parents who are abusive or neglectful, they are at great risk of becoming delinquent, anti-social and violent.

These are the children we have interviewed in prisons and youth detention centers serving sentences for assault and murder. In understanding their lives, we see clearly the value of our conceptual toolbox. When we use the periscope of social maps, we can see the negative world view they carry around. One of the things that increases the risk for the active/aggressive child is lack of positive attachment and feelings of being cared for; when emotionally abandoned, these children are at high risk. Difficulty in articulating their feelings positively further increases the risk. And inability to engage in an inner dialogue that illuminates emotions and allows a buffer between feeling and acting may put them on the road to aggressive crime.

In contrast to highly sensitive children, active/aggressive children are likely to be *under*responsive to the sensations of the world. They hunger for sensation in many situations that would be quite filling to others. They seek out newer and greater sensations, and their hunger manifests itself as fearlessness to danger, insensitivity to the feelings of others, and an apparent immunity to the corrective effects of punishment. When we employ the Geiger counter of social toxicity, we see that this is a dangerous combination. The danger of what these sensation-seeking kids can find in our society is awesome: lethal drugs, the availability of deadly weapons, and desensitizing and dehumanizing video games, for example.

These children need parents who show warmth and affection, set limits, and communicate clearly what those limits are. This communication needs to be through physical limit-setting as well as through words. Such youngsters need consistency in not having their behavior control their parents. Active/aggressive children tend to be clumsy when it comes to interpersonal emotions. They need coaching on how to see and respond to social and emotional cues, both positive and negative ones. They need to be "tamed" through consistent and firm limit-setting that is at the same time nurturing and gentle.

Active/aggressive children need parents who can recognize the vulnerability beneath the anger. That's not easy, but it is wise. Again, the parent needs to use words to offer such children a consciousness about their intense inner world. "Right now you seem to be like a volcano, ready to explode," the parent says. "Remember, we practiced breathing deeply and thinking about peaceful scenes when the volcano is ready to blow? Let's do that now together."

Parents should not try to "break" these children because that is likely only to suppress the aggression until the balance of power shifts within the home (most teens who assault their parents fit this pattern) or until it can be taken out on weaker kids outside the home (through bullying). And, some parents will need outside help to manage this process. Without it, the mishandled active/aggressive child can become an antisocial, delinquent, and violent teenager.

The stakes are high. Each temperamental type carries with it special challenges and opportunities for parents and all the other adults who matter—teachers, aunts, uncles, grandparents, and neighbors. Meeting those challenges is where the fate of vulnerable children rises or falls.

Now That We Know, What Can We Do?

Once we move away from blame, a whole new world opens up. As the Zen master Thich Nhat Hanh reminds us, "Blaming never helps," whether it is blaming others, blaming ourselves, or blaming our children for being the boy or girl he or she is. Patience, understanding, and appropriate responses—that is what has a chance to help. Stanley Greenspan captures this nicely when he entitles the first chapter of his book "You're Not the Cause, but You Can Be the Solution." Moving beyond assigning or feeling blame is liberating and empowering; it turns our attention to what we can do to help guide our children on a positive path and to support parents, no matter what their child's temperament.

When it comes to dealing with temperamentally difficult children, there are four crucial things for us to do. First, we must know our children as they are, not as we would like them to be. We must use the conceptual tools of child psychology. One of the virtues of thinking like a scientist is that it permits us to discipline ourselves as we observe others. It means not imposing preconceptions or bias or getting caught up in what actually is coincidence but may appear to be something else in the fervor of the mind to make sense of things.

Greenspan's book provides a good approach to this, a temperament-rating scale to help parents see their children more accurately. His approach is useful for children of any age. It helps parents separate assumptions from realities, hopes from facts, expectations from objective assessments. Even when their children are teenagers, it can be useful as a way of focusing on how they started life and how those early childhood patterns are evident years later, how a teenager is responding to high school, dating, career choices, and the temptations of drugs, alcohol, and sex.

Second, we must know ourselves. Let's not forget that we adults have temperaments underlying our personalities too. We, too, can have tendencies to be fussy, self-absorbed, defiant, inattentive, and aggressive, and we can be highly sensitive or detached, lethargic or hyperactive, emotionally unresponsive or relatively insensitive.

What parents bring to the child development equation is important because it shapes the way we offer alternative pathways for children, particularly challenging children. In her book *The*

Highly Sensitive Person: How to Thrive When the World Over-whelms You, psychologist Elaine Aron outlines the great challenges faced by highly sensitive parents. Highly sensitive parents must develop a very high level of self-awareness and self-control to deal with a challenging child. Knowledge is power, and knowing your own temperamental strengths and weaknesses is the first step toward mastering yourself so that you can be a more effective parent.

What is more, we must not forget that a large proportion of temperament is inherited. The genetic links between parents and their biological children mean that the odds of a child who is challenging being born to a parent who is challenging are greater than if the children and parents were matched up randomly. Thus, some families get a double dose of HSP—a parent and a child who are both highly sensitive.

Our children are our children, for better or worse, in sickness and in health. In her book *The Nurture Assumption*, child development specialist Judith Harris speaks of this link as one of the important sources of parental influence on children. The genetically transmitted features of temperament shape the life experiences of parents *and* children.

This heightens the need for self-awareness, because it is often precisely the attributes that we struggle against or don't like in ourselves that we have greatest difficulty accepting and dealing with in our children. Spiritual teacher Shakti Gawain prods us humorously on this point in her book *Awakening: A Daily Guide to Conscious Living*. She tells us that the more we try to push these things in a closet and lock the door to keep them away from us, the more they push back to get out and fall out in front of us. Everything wants to be loved, accepted, and included, and the more we deny these things about ourselves, the more they haunt us. Ironically, then, it is in accepting them that we find the first step toward changing them, in ourselves and our children.

We must understand this second point in light of the third,

however. Biology is *not* destiny. With rare exceptions, temperament affects only the probabilities, the odds that a child will
head in a particular direction. Temperament is only one factor
in the developmental equation. Once we accept this reality, we
can move toward change.

While temperament stems from innate characteristics, it need
not be immutable, locked in, and fixed. Some children are temperamentally predisposed to be fearful when confronted with
new things. Yet guided experiences can mute and even alter that
disposition, and dramatically reduce its role in the child's future
behavior and experience of the world. In short, enlightened action can change fear's place in a child's social map. Greenspan
is even more optimistic. He notes that "early care, in fact, not
only can change a child's behavior and personality, but can also
change the way a child's nervous system works" (p. 3).

Just as children can learn to compensate for their temperamental challenges, so can parents. And doing so—the creation
of self-awareness and transforming consciousness—is important if challenging children are to do well in the world. That's
good news for parents. Psychologist Daniel Goleman finds developing a package of social skills and psychological abilities
is crucial to life success. He outlines the elements of this complete package, which goes beyond IQ, in his book *Emotional
Intelligence*. Some children acquire these skills and abilities
more readily than others, but almost every child can get there if
the social environment—and in the beginning that mainly
means parents—carefully lays the groundwork with a keen
awareness of temperament.

Fourth, we can accept every child even as we seek to shape
and direct that child. A quarter of a century ago, anthropologist
Ronald Rohner studied rejection in cultures around the world.
In his book *They Love Me, They Love Me Not*, he found that in
every culture, rejected children are more likely to develop
whatever social and psychological pathologies are at issue in

that society. This connection was so strong, he said, that rejection was a "psychological malignancy," an emotional cancer.

How do we go about the difficult process of accepting the child absolutely while at the same time guiding the child? It's easy if the child is a model citizen, of course. Remember that Thomas and Chess found that only 10 percent of infants rated "easy" had significant problems by the time they were in elementary school. It is easier to convey acceptance to these children than it is to the difficult children, 70 percent of whom developed such problems. It's not easy to accept these children, but it can be done. Rohner's research tells us it must be done. How? We believe the starting point is spiritual, because every child is a spiritual being and that insight leads toward acceptance.

The Spiritual Foundation for Acceptance

Our goal is to discover the spiritual being before us in the challenging child. It is useful to consider how other people accept children who deviate from conventional ideas of what is normal in ways more dramatic than those dealt with by Stanley Greenspan. Let's consider two examples, the child with a physical or mental disability and the gay or lesbian child. Each makes special demands on parents; each challenges some parents' ability to accept. Some parents have great difficulty accepting a child with a mental or physical disability; others welcome such a child. And some parents have great difficulty accepting a child born with a predisposition to homosexuality, while others can accept that readily. Some parents could accept either child; some neither.

The fact is, some parents accept their children as they are, no matter what. Many of those who manage to rise to the occasion do so through spiritual awareness, even if they don't use those words. Spiritual awareness is very democratic, in the sense that it validates every person for his or her intrinsic value. This spiritual connection gives us a perspective larger than ourselves, one that helps us move away from rejection toward acceptance.

To be sure, the containers in which we encounter our spiritual essence vary greatly. Some are broken and damaged. Some are so different from ourselves that we have trouble empathizing with them, or even acknowledging them as fully human. Some people cannot see the spiritual nature inside the physically or mentally disabled child. But others can. Marvelous examples abound in the world of adoption and foster care. We recall with reverent awe Marge, who with her husband, Robert, adopted four children, each with significant disabilities—multiple sclerosis, Down's syndrome, extreme hyperactivity disorder, and mental retardation. Their lives were dominated by the daily challenges of caring for these children. But each of the children was a sacred spirit to these wonderful people.

With mindfulness and self-awareness, parents can overcome fear of difference and slowly come to accept the disabled child and the homosexual child. This fact provides a window of opportunity to see that the same is true of the varieties of challenging children identified by Stanley Greenspan.

Temperament is really about the diversity of containers in which a child's true essence comes to us. Their physical vessels differ in temperament as they do in their physical and mental abilities and sexual orientation. Our goal is always to find a way to accept and love the spiritual being while at the same time smoothing the way for the physical child to make his way in the world, morally, emotionally, socially, economically, and politically.

Staying in the Zone

Childhood is like a book with many chapters. In each chapter, there are multiple possible stories for each child, a range of possible behaviors in each situation. The issue in each situation is what the child can do alone and what the child can do with help. Alone, a shy five-year-old may find it impossible to enter the kindergarten classroom and initiate social interaction. With a caring and astute teacher as a guide, carefully smoothing the way, the same child can start school. This sort of facilitation and enabling are crucial to Greenspan's approach to helping challenging children succeed in the world.

But there is more to it. The Russian psychologist Lev Vygotsky provided the classic thinking about how developmental facilitation takes place. Two of his concepts are important for all parents, but particularly for parents of challenging children: The Zone of Proximal Development and Scaffolding.

The Zone of Proximal Development signifies the range of possibilities between what the child can do alone and what the child can do with help. The distance between these two things is that "zone." Vygotsky's breakthrough was to see that the more the child is "in the zone," the better his or her development, because development is fundamentally a social process. The young child says, "Car go!" while running a toy across the floor. What is the developmentally stimulating response that moves the child into the zone? It is something along the lines of "That's right, honey. The car is going. And where do you think the car is going?" This validates the child while at the same time offering the next developmental step—elaborating the language and stimulating new thoughts and actions.

Similarly, Scaffolding is about the building of ever-more-complex patterns of thought and behavior from more simple forms. Like the scaffold a painter erects outside a building before starting to work, the child's scaffold provides a basis for working on thoughts, feelings, and behavior. It gives the child a basis on which to build, something in which to trust.

The Issue of Trust

Trust is one of the building blocks of human development. Lack of trust comes from inside as well as outside the child. Trust requires confidence that one is competent, that one is justified in self-acceptance. Children may fear loss of control over overwhelming impulses or feelings that they view as unacceptable. This provokes a crisis of trust.

Children may also fear that such a loss of control would result in losing a relationship with an important person. For example, if a child perceives his parent as rejecting him because of his anger, then the child could fear that playing aggressive symbolic scenarios would lead to unleashing an explosive outburst that would alienate him from the parent.

Many maltreated children seem to learn to be distrustful as a coping technique. They are reluctant to relinquish this strategy, and will do so only after repeated testing to ensure their safety and the reliability of the adult. Other children may be overly trusting of even unfamiliar adults becuase of their craving for attention and nurturance, but this overeagerness may turn into disillusionment if the adult fails to live up to their exaggerated expectations.

When youngsters do not trust themselves because of something that has happened to them, they do not believe in their own capacity to be successful in the world. This, too, inhibits the process of development. As we noted in Chapter 2, psychoanalyst Erik Erikson identified the early development of trust versus mistrust as a watershed in child development. It stands as an important consideration in understanding how well any child is doing in getting on with the business of growing up.

The issue of trust has important dimensions beyond the home and family, however, in which parents have a vital stake. Trust is one of the core issues in the school as well as the home. We have often pointed to the importance of the social environment in which children develop, and the crucial role of social toxicity, particularly for vulnerable, "psychologically asth-matic" children. The school is a primary setting in this regard. Of special importance in shaping the fate of challenging children is the degree to which the school promotes cooperation and acceptance. Social psychologist Elliot Aronson has spelled out the costs of corrosive competition and rejection in school for vulnerable children in his book *Nobody Left to Hate*. He goes beyond spelling out the problem to propose a well-grounded solution: the systematic introduction of cooperative structures in the classroom. His approach is called the Jigsaw Classroom, and his research demonstrates its success in channeling the social relationships among children into an acceptable direction by involving them in teams that demand and reward cooperation.

Conclusion

This chapter explored the special tasks faced by parents whose children are temperamentally challenging. Such children can try the patience of any ordinary parent. In contrast to easy children, difficult children demand an extraordinary amount of sensitivity and perseverance on the part of the parent, as well as social support from the whole environment around the parent. The parental compass helps guide them through this challenge. These children are best understood as "psychological asthmatics," and their fate depends in large measure on how well their parents do in accepting their child and then becoming a teacher to help the child learn how to transform himself or herself into an emotionally intelligent and mindful person.

Lesson: Every challenging child has a positive path if only parents have the wisdom from within and the support from the community needed to discover it and to be with the child on that path.

7

Aspiring to Be an Authority Figure in an Out-of-Control Society

What Have We Lost?

What is the measure of a generation? Demographers tend to talk about numbers of years, seeking some standard measure. But the novelist F. Scott Fitzgerald said that generations change when one wave of people defines themselves as being distinct from the wave before them. Others might go still further and say that there is a change of generations when both the new and the old group can't understand each other, perhaps even think the other is out of its mind.

These two approaches say that rather than some fixed number of years to mark the changing of generations, it is the sense of incredulity and lack of shared experiences that defines generations. This makes sense to us. When Jim talks about coming of age in the 1960s, Claire—who came of age in the 1970s—finds his experiences somewhat foreign. When music, movies, television programs, and historical references all become alien between two people of different ages, there is a generation gap. And the authors have that.

Sometimes the gaps between generations can be bridged. Reading Tom Brokaw's *The Greatest Generation*—about coming of age in the 1940s—we can relate, even feel nostalgia, for a time when people thought the world was simple, when children viewed it in child-size terms, not with the apparent sophistication of today's kids. Even in childhood in the 1950s, things *seemed* simpler and safer. The people across the street got furious if you accidentally hit a ball onto their lawn, but no one ever thought of suing anybody over it. The man down the street did some crazy things (like dressing up as the New Year's baby on New Year's Eve and then getting in an accident in his car and getting arrested), but the neighborhood kids didn't know he was an "alcoholic."

Having grown up fifteen years later, and in Canada, to Claire the cultural specifics of American childhood of the 1950s and adolescence of the 1960s seem alien. But the sense of safety and structure do not, rooted in a safe suburban neighborhood in a society with a strong ethic of caring and community. The authors share that with each other. But with our kids, who grew up in the 1980s and 1990s?

Sometimes we both feel like dinosaurs trying to explain what life was like before mammals when we talk to our children about the old days, they who know about divorce firsthand, who cannot avoid knowing about rape and murder and the other staples of the daily news, who know so much about AIDS, drugs, genocide, and sexual abuse. They who have come of age in the shadow of school massacres and Monica Lewinsky and the tabloid television shows.

What have we lost? Or more specifically, what have children

and parents lost? Put most simply, we have lost the belief that there is a positive, protective structure of authority in the lives of both children and parents. Children don't feel as safe as they once did, and they don't see a social order around them that provides safety and guidance. That's what they have lost. Parents don't feel as powerful as they once did, and they don't feel they have the authority their parents took for granted. That's what we have lost. The Gannett survey noted in Chapter 1 found that 82 percent of American adults believe children today are less respectful of their elders than in earlier generations. Alex Packer, the author of *How Rude! The Teenager's Guide to Good Manners, Proper Behavior and Not Grossing People Out* says, "I've been stunned by the collapse of civility." This may not be mere nostalgia for the good old days but may reflect more significant problems—for example, problems with trust.

The National Survey of Youth reported in 1973 that 40 percent of the country's 17-year-olds agreed with the statement "You can't be too careful in dealing with people." By 1992 it was 60 percent. In 1973, 35 percent of our youth agreed that "most people can be trusted." By 1992 it was down to 17 percent. Why this erosion of basic trust? One place to look is the civic cynicism of adults. In 1963, 77 percent of American adults agreed with the statement "You can count on the government to do the right thing most of the time." By 1993, the corresponding figure was 22 percent, and we find that many people actually laugh when presented with this statement. We think adult civic cynicism and youthful distrust are linked.

If God Is Dead, Who's in Charge?

The 1960s saw a remarkable change in the language of religious discourse in America. The central change was the assertion "God is dead." The God is dead "movement" was not really an atheist manifesto, but rather a lament that holiness was disappearing from our lives. The common expression "Is nothing sacred?" captures this. For parents and children, it is the decline of the sacred that is most important because with it comes an almost inevitable decline in the structure of adult authority.

Human beings have evolved to live in an orderly social system, one with firm, clear structures and lines of authority. Take this away, and we are threatened with chaos. An important part of social order derives from recognizing the sacred: to set limits, to define what is done and not done, to give a higher purpose. "God's in his heaven; all's right with the world," said the eighteenth-century poet Alexander Pope.

The issues of sacredness and authority are connected. At the extremes, we find that kids who kill typically demonstrate a kind of spiritual emptiness, and thus lack a sense of limits, reverence for life, and a deep sense of being connected to love. Parents who cannot parent with love also present such a spiritual emptiness. Religions that offer only fear and the prospect of punishment similarly fail.

Spirituality, not the suppressing force of divine power, is the key. It is a matter of manifesting love rather than fear of the "wrath of God" that makes a difference—a focus on being a Christlike person rather than a Christian, a Buddha rather than a Buddhist, for example. Research demonstrates that kids who are engaged in some kind of nonpunitive religion or spiritual faith tend to be buffered from many of the social pathologies that afflict American youth—drugs, violence, delinquency, irresponsible sex. It is not dogma or the fire-and-brimstone aspects of certain religions that protects kids, but the loving, compassionate aspects of which Martin Luther King, Jr. spoke so often. It's not parents who beat their children who have this authority, but parents who lead through positive example.

This, of course, is why kids *can* get their spiritual needs met outside the confines of organized religion, and why some kids inside do not. The key is building a strong sense of living in a meaningful universe governed by love, compassion, and something greater than oneself. Involving kids in activities that promote reverence for life, an ethic of caring, and a commitment to live with humility rather than arrogance—these are the keys to imbuing children and youth with the positive authority that universal love inspires. When the religious experience of children and youth is restricted to a punitive, authoritarian religion, they may end up with an ideology that rationalizes anger, hatred, and bigotry. Therefore, religion per se is not a catchall solution. Careful examination of the messages behind a particular religion or spiritual belief is key in determining the potential buffering benefits of faith in our children's lives.

How can parents develop a sense of authority that flows from an appreciation of the sacred? They can do so in part through how they live their own lives. Mahatma Gandhi spoke these powerfully guiding words: "You must be the change you wish to see in the world." The place to start transformation is always with ourselves. In his book *Care of the Soul,* theologian and counselor Thomas Moore offers some very practical guidance on how to recognize and nurture sacredness in day-to-day life, how to meet basic spiritual needs. His suggestions include taking the time to invest in family and personal rituals that recognize the deeper meanings rather than getting swept away with the mundane details of life.

Beyond cultivating the sacred, parents can recognize how badly children need to live within the protective cocoon of adult authority. One danger is that parents will be too intimate with their children, pals rather than parents. This intimacy is tempting for many parents, particularly single parents, or married parents who are emotionally disconnected from their spouses. Both groups may naturally gravitate to their children for meeting their emotional needs, sometimes without being consciously aware of it. Being a pal rather than a parent is particularly unwise in raising children who are temperamentally at risk, and who need a strong structure of authority to make it through their frustrating encounters with school and the world of peers.

And it is particularly difficult for stepparents, who may feel on shaky ground when it comes to authority—a feeling their stepchildren and even their spouses may share. In all these cases, it is tempting to turn to the child as a social equal, as an emotional partner (albeit it without any sexual content at all). But giving in to this temptation erodes the foundation of the authority parents need to do their job—and ultimately that children need to do theirs. Children need parents who can protect them, not simply older friends who happen to be Mom and Dad. Why? Because as we saw in Chapter 4, security is vitally important to them.

There is growing recognition of the need to provide children with security. One manifestation is the character-education movement, through organized efforts to promote in children the moral compass of character. Across the country, schools, civic groups, and religious organizations are mobilizing their efforts to concentrate on the character education of children. Educator Thomas Lickona is a leader in this effort. His book *Educating for Character: How Our Schools Can Teach Respect and Responsibility* lays out the rationale and some of the institutional policies and practices that encourage character development, done best as a collaboration of schools with the entire range of community actors—police, business, the faith community, and civic groups.

Programs like those of the Hyde Schools organize themselves around the need to place character at the center of the educational process. Hyde has even produced a parent program that reflects this approach. Through a series of workshops, The Biggest Job program seeks to help parents take moral charge of family life through ten principles. "Truth over harmony," "Principles over rules," "Attitude over aptitude," are the first three. The remaining seven speak to common issues parents face in understanding how to translate values into child behavior and

155

development—in short, into character. These approaches are worth exploring in any parent's efforts to find a basis for positive authority amid the chaos of modern society.

Learning from the Extremes

The most psychologically vulnerable kids in our society serve as weather vanes and social indicators of what is going on. They are our canaries in the coal mines. The most vulnerable kids act like social Geiger counters themselves, albeit usually unconsciously. In their problem behavior they show us clearly what is out there in our socially toxic environment, for these most vulnerable kids will be as bad as the social environment shows, teaches, and permits. If we know how to look, we can see it in every message they send with their out-of-control behavior, their wanton aggressiveness, their foul mouths, their blindness to any controlling authority except force.

We live in a society out of control. It is tempting to think that this affects *only* the most vulnerable among us—boys and girls in prison, mental hospitals, residential treatment centers, or detention facilities. But that comforting belief would be a mistake. Kids already caught by or in the system may act out flamboyantly, but they are not alone. Gangs are cropping up in the suburbs. There are documented reports of middle-class teenagers carrying weapons to school. In a third-grade classroom in a middle-class suburb of Chicago, a third of the children told us they knew where to get a gun "if we needed one."

There is growing national concern about the widespread use of drugs in an effort to control the behavior of troubled and troubling kids. It is not a simple issue, however. There are kids who need help from pharmacology to make a go of it—some 3 to 5 percent of kids are affected by problems with attention deficits and between 2 to 3 percent are affected by depression. Since both conditions often elicit the prescribing of drugs when the sufferer is an adult, it should come as no surprise that drugs are prescribed for youngsters too. Drugs do play a positive role in some cases. The Surgeon General's report on children's mental health makes this clear.

This is not to say there are no concerns—for example, the lack of data showing the long-term safety of such drugs with young children and the fact that the trend toward managed care means that a high priority is given to treatment strategies that avoid long-term and costly in-depth interventions in favor of simple "silver bullet" approaches that can cut costs. This is a terrible concern, when there is growing evidence that some drugs prescribed for children can trigger extreme adverse reactions—including violent outbursts in some cases.

When prescribed for very specific conditions after a thorough exploration of psychological and social conditions in the child's life, and with appreciation that the principal interventions needed for such children are behavioral and intellectual, some drugs make sense. However, the overall pattern in the United States does not generally meet these standards. There is too much prescription, too little in-depth diagnosis, too little effort to help the social environment change to meet the legitimate needs of children, and too few professionals with the psychiatric knowledge needed to justify the use of drugs as they are currently employed. And weak schools seem unable to handle difficult children effectively through social and psychological measures.

We hear far too many stories like the one told by Lisa, the mother of a very difficult boy:

> I have quite a few friends whose kids go to the same school as my boy, and I would watch their kids go through school and have their doctors say "Put him on Ritalin." So they would come to me because they knew a little bit about what I had been going through. That is how I chose to become an advocate for these parents. I would go to school and say "Look, why do you want this child to be put on Ritalin?"

and the teacher would reply, "Well, because he talks too much." He's just being a *boy,* I think! I felt that I made a difference in some parents' lives. If I could prevent just one person from going through what Eric had gone through, and what I have gone through, it would be worth so much to me. I even made up handbooks about what the laws were in my state for a special child. A child deserves to have a good education, even if he or she is learning disabled. I know a couple of parents who were ready to put their child on Ritalin, and I would try to tell them about it. I would say, "You don't know anything about Ritalin. Go to the nurse's office and get her book on medications and read up on it. When you find out what the symptoms are and about the long-term effects of this drug, then you may think twice about it." I remember one particular parent to whom I suggested she go in the classroom and talk to her child's teacher to find out exactly what was going on in the school. The parent did, and she stood up for her son, and after talking with the teacher, the kid did not end up being put on medication, and he's doing fine. It's such a fight! It's a fight you shouldn't have to fight. Teachers are supposed to be trained in how to handle a different child. But some of the teachers I dealt with were so inept in dealing with children who didn't respond to their liking—especially my son's first-grade teacher, who had him sitting at the very front of the room and paddled him every day and told him he was so bad. It's unbelievable in this day and age, but this is a teacher who is tenured and probably still there at that school.

A Case Study: High School Size

After their homes, perhaps the biggest immediate influences on youth are their peer groups and the schools they attend. One often-overlooked feature of schools, most notably the high schools, that contributes to the difficulties parents face in raising teenagers today is their size. Put simply, big high schools encourage spectatorship and the "herd feeling" rather than participation, and exclude all but a small proportion of their students from leadership roles and other developmentally enhancing activities. Small schools leave the majority of students at loose ends and the most vulnerable youth ripe for the destructive pressures of the socially toxic environment.

By contrast, small schools enhance affirmation and identity because they draw kids into participation and leadership, offer challenges that stimulate the development of competence, and monitor behavior more effectively. All these effects are strongest for the students most at risk for alienation and dropping out, the "academically marginal" students. Generally, parents who are coping with such a child at home have a natural ally in the small school and a natural enemy in the large school.

A visit to the smallest public high school in Nassau County, outside New York City, after a thirty-year absence revealed that even academically and socially, marginal kids had a sense of belonging there. They said things like, "It's like a family here. You know you can count on everyone. You know everyone." They said, "You can't get away with anything here. Someone always notices what you are doing." That's a good recipe for positive development in teenagers, to act so the kids will think: "People care about me, and they prove it by paying attention to what I do—both the good and the bad." That's about character. Remember that as we proceed.

Most of the important research on high school size was done in the 1950s and 1960s, and it documented the superiority of small schools in providing a positive environment for teenagers. This research—much of it conducted by psychologists Roger Barker and Paul Gump and their colleagues in Kansas—found that the large school tends to discourage students from meaningful participation in its social and extracurricular activities and thus to diminish their sense of personal ownership for what happens in the school and their sense of responsibility. However, just as this evidence was becoming available, social forces and deliberate policy were closing and consolidating small schools in favor of big ones.

Barker and Gump demonstrated that although the large school provides more settings in which students can act, there are proportionately more kids to fill those settings (thus the large school is "overmanned"). Small high schools, in contrast, have more settings than kids to fill them (and thus are "undermanned"). For example, although the large school may have both a chorus and a glee club, together these two settings can accommodate only a small proportion of the student body, so it is still hard for any given student (particularly a student with little talent) to get into either activity. A small high school probably has just one vocal group, but is apt to be so hungry for voices that any student willing to make the effort to participate will be welcomed.

The kinds of satisfactions reported by students differed in the small school versus the large school. Researchers found that students from small schools reported satisfaction clustering around the development of responsibility, competence, challenge, and a sense of identity. That makes sense. They were being drawn into positions of responsibility and activity on behalf of pro-social goals—putting on concerts, organizing meetings, practicing and working in teams in preparation for competing in athletic events. This is the stuff of which healthy environments are made—particularly for kids who do not yet possess all the internal resources and motivation needed to succeed *despite* the social environment.

In contrast, most students in large high schools emphasized vicarious, passive enjoyment: watching the elite perform and generally feeling part of a nameless, faceless crowd—what

160

Barker and Gump called the "herd feeling." This may have been tolerable fifty years ago, when there were fewer kids coming to school loaded with the family risk factors of separation and divorce, when they did not encounter the same temptations of drugs, when the mass media were tame by today's standards, when the larger structures of adult authority were largely intact, and when kids who dropped out of high school could still get on track occupationally. But today? Today the costs of being an at-risk kid are much greater, and the need to go to a school that compensates for the larger toxic society is dramatically greater.

In large high schools, at-risk kids are superfluous; in the small high schools, they are needed. It's not a matter of the teachers, staff, and student leaders in the small school being nicer or having been to "inclusiveness workshops." Nor is it a matter of the teachers, staff, and student leaders in the large school being mean or exclusionary. It is an issue of social context, a manifestation of the human ecology of the school. Psychologist Rudolf Moos uses the term "the principle of progressive conformity" to describe how people tend to become what their environment elicits and rewards. The big school elicits and rewards passivity and marginal involvement among most students, and leadership and activity only among the elite. The small school elicits and rewards participation and responsibility among the whole student body as a matter of necessity.

What is big and what is small? Researchers working in the 1950s and early 1960s concluded that after a school exceeds 500 students in grades 9 through 12 it quickly takes on the dynamics of bigness. From 1955 to 1975 the average size of our high schools grew from about 500 to about 1,500 students. Just walk into most large high schools, and you can see and feel what the researchers were documenting half a century ago. Many look and feel like factories—or even worse, like prisons. Elaborate security systems are in place to *try* to keep track of students. But even so, the schools leak students all day long.

Look at the yearbook and see how little active participation there is for most students. Look at the data on dropping out and delinquency among the high-risk students.

In contrast, visit a small school like the one we saw in Nassau County. No look of a war zone. No security guards. No students unaccounted for. All this despite the presence of at-risk youth and marginal students. One reason many parents are under siege today is the fact that when their kids go to school, they get another dose of social toxicity rather than an antidote.

But even small schools today are not immune to the social forces that undermine the successful development of our kids. Educational psychologist Ellen deLara undertook an in-depth study of how safe kids felt in a small high school in a rural part of New York State. As it happened, she conducted the first part of her study in the fall of the 1998–1999 school year and completed it at the end of the spring term. This permitted her to observe the impact of the Columbine High School shootings on the perceived safety of the school.

What she found is disturbing. Prior to Columbine, 82 percent of the kids said, "I can count on it that the teachers or other adults would stop someone from hurting me or anyone else in the classroom." After Columbine, only 60 percent of the kids agreed. Even the small high school is vulnerable to the corrosive effects of social toxicity, but the small school does have a lot going for it—for the kids who attend and the parents who send them there. The small school is an asset for the community and for families.

Recognizing the Assets in Community, Family, and Children

One hopeful trend is the growing appeal of movements in schools, families, and communities to recognize and promote the building of cultural, social, and psychological strengths in the lives of children. One of the leaders in this approach is the Search Institute, in Minneapolis, Minnesota. Based on their research with schools and communities across the nation, they offer a list of forty "Developmental Assets."

Their research shows that the more developmental assets a child has, the more that child is likely to live effectively, as measured by being less likely to be involved with drugs and alcohol, to be sexually irresponsible, or to be violent and in trouble at school and in the community. In short, the more assets, the more the child is likely to respond to the positives toward which adult authority is directed. The purpose of adult authority is not control for control's sake, nor power for power's sake. Its purpose is to guide and protect children in ways that promote successful development. A brief look at the Search Institute's list of assets confirms this.

The forty assets are grouped into eight categories: Support, Empowerment, Boundaries and Expectations, Constructive Use of Time, Commitment to Learning, Positive Values, Social Competencies, and Positive Identity. Let's take a look at some of them. For a start, the Boundaries and Expectations category includes:

Family Boundaries: "Family has clear rules and consequences, and monitors the young person's whereabouts."

School Boundaries: "School provides clear rules and consequences."

Neighborhood Boundaries: "Neighbors take responsibility for monitoring young people's behavior."

Adult Role Models: "Parent(s) and other adults model responsible behavior."

Positive Peer Influence: "Young person's best friends model responsible behavior."

High Expectations: "Both parent(s) and teachers encourage the young person to do well."

The emphasis on kids being embedded within a positive structure of adult authority is clear here, but is it also evident in other asset clusters? For example, within Constructive Use of Time we find the following assets: "Young person spends three or more hours per week in sports, clubs, or organizations at school and/or in community organizations." Among Positive Values we find "Young person accepts and takes personal responsibility." Within Positive Identity we find "Young person reports that 'my life has a purpose'" and among Support is "Young person receives support from three or more non-parent adults."

How important are these assets in predicting which young people will live up to ideals of good behavior and respect the positive adult authority inherent in the rules of good conduct and character? In their research including communities across the country, among kids with 0 to 10 assets, the rate of drug abuse is 42 percent, the rate of problem alcohol use is 53 percent, and violence is 61 percent. In contrast, among kids with 31–40 assets, the rate of drug abuse is 1 percent, the rate of problem alcohol use is 3 percent, and the rate of violence is 6 percent.

On the positive side, for kids with 0 to 10 assets, the rate of school success is 7 percent, maintaining good health is 25 percent, and delaying gratification is 27 percent, whereas for kids with 31 to 40 assets, the corresponding figures are 53 percent, 88 percent, and 72 percent. The picture is clear: The more assets youths have, the more likely that they are living up to the kinds of ideals we as parents and citizens hope for.

We return to the implications of these findings at the end of this book. But it is worth noting here that youths who don't fit the typical patterns are particularly interesting. A significant proportion of the kids who have only 0 to 10 assets are still non-violent and drug free, and there are kids among those with 31 to 40 assets who are violent and who use hard drugs. The former exemplify resilience; the latter might be described as "asset resistant." Both groups are important stories, and we will return to each later.

Using Our Tools

How can we assert authority in an out-of-control world? For some, the obvious answer is the exercise of sheer power. The movement to try to reform delinquent youths by sending them to boot camp is one example. "Get tough on them," this approach tells us. But the failure of boot camps is now well-documented, and state governments are closing them down in the wake of nationwide research findings showing that they are no more effective than conventional youth prisons, often less so. In any case, they are particularly prone to abuse.

Reading accounts of this retreat from the boot-camp model in an article by journalist David Krajicek in *Youth Today* and again in a *New York Times* article on January 2, 2000, we were reminded of a story told by the principal of a tough high school. Finding himself with extra funds in his school security budget, he prepared to hire an additional security guard to augment the two already on staff, both of whom were physically powerful men. His choice for the third guard position? A five-foot-tall grandmother with strong ties to and respect in the community. Her authority was unquestionable, and she emerged as the most effective force for authority in the hallways of the school. Her authority stemmed from her social assets, and authority is always the most effective social power.

The need for security in an out-of-control world can lead us to strategies that actually justify and increase aggression and violence in our families and our communities as we mistakenly fight fire with fire. But that's a self-defeating path, as most of the world's great spiritual teachers tell us. Recall Buddha's words: "You will not be punished for your anger, you will be punished by your anger." Jesus said, "The meek shall inherit the earth." Mahatma Gandhi called it "soul force," and Martin Luther King brought it home to America. As Wayne Dyer puts it in his book *Real Magic,* "All that you fight weakens you; all that you support empowers you."

So what can parents do? The microscope of our ecological perspective helps us see that the impact of what parents do depends, in part, on what else is going on in the larger society. This is what social context is all about. Thus, for example, a study of permissive child-rearing practices conducted in the 1920s by psychologist Percival Symonds revealed that it worked, producing the most competent and positive children. But a study of permissive child rearing by psychologist Diana Baumrind in the 1970s revealed that it no longer worked so well.

Baumrind found that permissive parents produced children who were less competent and positive than children reared by parents who maintained a higher level of authority; but it was authority coupled with flexibility—listening to the child's point of view but retaining decision-making power. How do we reconcile these discrepant results, the findings of Symonds in the 1920s and Baumrind in the 1970s? To begin with, the social environment outside the home in the twenties was highly authoritarian. In such a context parents could "afford" to be permissive at home. In fact, it may have been beneficial to children to have a more easygoing family life when school and community were so regimented and dictatorial.

By the seventies, however, things had changed. The world around the family was becoming ever more chaotic, and kids needed more structure at home, not less. Thus, the authoritative strategy made sense and showed more positive results. Further support for this interpretation comes from contemporary studies that examine what works for parents today in different social environments. Research conducted by psychologist Al Baldwin and his colleagues shows that less democratic and more restrictive parenting works better for parents in dangerous inner-city neighborhoods, while in the relatively safe environments of the affluent suburbs, a more democratic, less restrictive approach succeeds better. Context is always important, and understanding yours is crucial for developing an effective parenting strategy when it comes to authority—indeed, in every aspect of child development.

We must also remember the importance of using our calculator of risk and opportunity to sort out the complicated question of who is vulnerable and who is resilient. The more risk factors are stacked against a child and a parent, and the fewer the available assets, the greater the need to compensate with greater strength to prove to children that the parent is indeed strong enough to protect them. The more obvious resources a parent has, the easier it is to convince a child that the parent is powerful. When our risk-opportunity calculator shows a positive balance (opportunities outnumber risks), parents are on firm ground; when the reverse is true, authority is called into question.

Always recognize the importance of temperament. When we look through the periscope of temperament, we see that some children are predisposed to be resistant to authority. They don't respond well to easygoing, informal discipline—it rolls off their backs like water off a duck. In the most extreme cases, children seem almost impervious to conventional authority. These are likely to go down the tubes in a chaotic family with weak lines of authority.

But such children may thrive in a highly structured home environment from their earliest days, a home where adults are consistent, unified, and unrelenting in insisting that the child walk a straight path; a loving, accepting home, but one imbued with authority. Without it, these children are likely to lose themselves in antisocial behavior, particularly when our social

Geiger counter is reading a high level of social toxicity around them.

For the temperamentally vulnerable child, both the abusive and the unstructured path can lead to the severe problems we discussed earlier: conduct disorder, oppositional defiance, antisocial personality disorder, and even, ultimately, the nightmare of psychopathic behavior. Are such children doomed? We don't think so, but the odds are stacked against their parents (and every other adult who is responsible for them).

Such parents and other adults will need all the support they can get, and spiritual anchoring may be the key. What else is strong enough to stand against the combined power of their vulnerability and social toxicity?

Perhaps more than most kids, temperamentally high-risk children need a strong spiritual foundation to provide a clear and positive sense of limits and authority. Involve them in religious experiences that teach reverence for life and the need to live a life disciplined by awareness of a Higher Power. Pray for them. Pray with them. Use techniques of mindfulness to create an order that is seamlessly internal and external at the same time. Spiritual authority is the deepest and strongest authority there is. Cultivate it, and use the soul force it produces to protect children and youth from each other and from themselves, as well as from the noxious influences of our toxic society.

Remember that children live inside and by their social maps. The structure of adult authority provides the rules of the road and the traffic signs. The authors' awareness of multiculturalism reminds us that each culture has its own unique sources and language of authority. In South Africa, a counselor told us of his success in dealing with out-of-control youth by speaking to them of the ancient tribal code that each boy knew but which at first seemed to have no place in the modern world they inhabited. Yet it could be recalled and employed to good purpose.

Parents and educators in America are developing an appreciation of the importance of cultural tradition and ritual as resources in combating social toxicity. Research in the United States shows that the self-esteem of African American children is enhanced when adults communicate knowledge and pride in their heritage as an antidote to the psychologically corrosive effects of racism. The high school principal who hired an elderly grandmother as a security guard, a dignified lady known and respected in the community, knew she could speak to the students with the unassailable authority of a tribal elder.

Some challenges to parents are universal in our society. There are some strategies for dealing with these common issues that can get us started toward increasing children's sense that they live in a world in which there *is* a protective structure of adult authority. Regulate television and movie watching, starting at an early age. The American Academy of Pediatrics recommends no television at all until a child is 4 years of age. Monitor what children do watch and how they reflect what they watch in their clothing, their language, and the way they treat each other. Encourage positive media experiences, positive language, and positive peer relations. Positive heroes can be very useful for children—and their parents. What they watch matters.

Use discipline that teaches love and self-control rather than force to punish children. As sociologist Murray Straus points out in his book *Beating the Devil Out of Them,* hitting children to discipline them has side effects later on in life, including problems with aggression and sexual intimacy. It's often hard to see this at the lower ends of the spectrum—"normal spanking"—but there is a connection. What's the answer? Recognize that alternatives to hitting do exist, and they work without the nasty side effects. Start early by using words and nonviolent behavior control to set limits and impose real, understandable consequences. Apply them consistently. Consistency and structure lead to predictability, and predictability is an important teacher for children.

We can join together with other parents so that we all are enforcing the same expectations for behavior and TV watching. Here's an area where individualism can make things more difficult. Surveys show that parents want to control TV access themselves, not have government do the job through state censorship. But the more there is a consensus among parents in a school, a child care center, or a neighborhood, the easier it is to get compliance from kids. Look to the PTA, churches, and other groups for leadership and support.

We can work to make schools safety zones for children. Help educators to make schools smaller so that they can exert more personalized and thus effective discipline and deter guns and gangs. Parent volunteers in school hallways can help create a positive social climate. Support violence prevention and conflict resolution programs at all levels—from preschool through high school—to remake the culture of childhood and adolescence. Involve children and youth in lobbying efforts to promote gun control and disarmament. These efforts help persuade kids that adults are strong and are strongly committed to safety and security.

Conclusion

Children and youth need to live with a structure of adult authority, in the family, the school, and the community. When the world outside the home seems out of control, parents must communicate authority to their children. So long as they receive strong messages of love and profound acceptance, children learn to live within limits in society by practicing it at home.

Lesson: Parents must establish their authority by connecting with the authority resources of their culture, because anarchy and chaos undermine the development of their children.

8

Parenting in a Material World

Time Is Money?

Economists have found a way to measure everything in dollars and cents. In this way of looking at the world, child rearing and education contribute to economic productivity and translate into human capital investments. From an economic point of view, the time parents invest in their children increases human capital and therefore takes on economic value. Parents and teachers are using time and energy to improve the quality of their "products"—the children in their families and the students in their classrooms. This is crucial to the process of converting a human organism into a human being. This is the economy of time.

The economy of time is very important in childhood and in child rearing. How will children spend their time? Will they invest it in education or squander it playing video games? Will they spend it with adults or with their peers? Every decision has implications for their well-being and the quality of the social environment. Every decision has an impact on human capital, now and in the future.

If children spend their time reading and doing their homework, in community service, taking music and art lessons, or playing sports, all society benefits. These activities are assets in the Search Institute's approach to enhancing youth development that we introduced in Chapter 7. If children instead use their time mostly watching television, obsessing about their next toy or doll or video game, or cruising shopping malls and listening to pop music, we all suffer through lost human capital investment. The money kids spend may give the economy a short-term boost, but this reaps a short-term payoff. The same goes for parents. The more time we spend in positive activities with our kids rather than shopping or watching television, the better the family's "product" in the long run, and the greater the gain in human capital.

What are our criteria for making decisions about spending, investing, or wasting time—in short, about the experience of each present moment? One criterion is what makes us happy. Another is the cost of alternatives, because time spent one way is not available for another. What's it going to be, an hour spent playing ball with your children or an hour spent watching television? Why not do both, and have your cake and eat it too? These are economic questions, questions about choices and investments. But the economics of family life and child rearing are not simple, and they operate in two different economies, not one. As parents, we must teach our children to live well in both and to understand the differences between the two.

Two Economies

You check up on your son's brushing his teeth. You remind your daughter to wash her hands before she comes to the dinner table. The old lady next door takes care of your son when he gets home from school while you and your partner work. You drop the kids off at school on your way to work. Your son builds his sister a soapbox derby car from some lumber and old wheels he finds in the garage. Your daughter knits you a sweater. Your neighbor shows you how to fix the front steps of your house. You show his wife how to bake a cake. Your kids team up with the kids down the street to put on a puppet show for the neighborhood. Your son and the neighbor's kid organize a soapbox derby race on the block. All these things represent an exchange of goods and services, or economic activity. Yet they are invisible in conventional economic accounting systems. None appear in the government's calculations of the Gross National Product (GNP), since no dollars and cents change hands in the transactions.

What will it take for such goods and services to show up in the GNP, to become economically visible? You drive your kids to the dentist's office, where the nurse teaches them how to use a new electric toothbrush ($100 for the visit and $99 for the electric toothbrush). You pay a family day care provider to take care of your youngest child each weekday afternoon ($100 per week). The private bus service picks your daughter up each morning to take her to school, door to door ($75 per week). You go with your older son and his younger brother to pick out a battery-operated minicar at the toy store ($275). Your daughter buys you a new sweater for your birthday ($25). The neighbor refers you to a carpenter who fixes the front steps ($85), and in return your partner buys his wife a cake at the bakery ($10). The kids down the street invite your kids into their house to catch the Disney Channel on cable TV ($29.95 per month), and in return, your son lets them try his new video game cartridge ($50.50). Total contribution to the GNP: $849.45.

The Gross National Product measures the cash transactions involving goods and services that take place in a society. The term for this is the *monetarized economy.* The GNP does not measure the activities in which no money changes hands, what is called the *nonmonetarized economy*. But a great deal of work, production, and business is done in the parallel economy, particularly when it comes to the goods and services that really matter in the development of children. According to some estimates, for most of our nation's history, more than 90 percent of basic health care and child care took place within families and neighborhoods (that is, with the people and in the places where no money changes hands). Such goods and services are no less real than those that have a dollar sign attached to them, even though they are largely invisible in conventional models of economic accounting. As a result, if we simply shift activities from the nonmonetarized economy into the economy that attaches a dollar price to them, what may appear as economic growth may only be a switch in accounting.

What is more, this process can hide real losses and make them appear as gains. For example, in some areas, the deteriorating quality of public drinking water has created a market for selling bottled water. Some enterprising business even had the idea of selling oxygen in special booths along the streets of cities suffering from air pollution.

The general model is this: If children can no longer swim free in the local lake and must use a swimming pool because the lake has become polluted, their families must pay money for the pool use, and the GNP shows an increase. However, there may actually be a decrease in enjoyment, because some families may not be able to afford the price of what was once free. That puts pressure on all families to generate the cash income needed to participate, and it accentuates the social costs of being poor—that is, of having too few dollars to buy into the normal activities of your society.

The minute some thing or activity moves or changes into the cash economy, it becomes a possible source of financial profit to someone. When this happens, a whole new set of actors is drawn into the decision making about what we do and with whom. It's no longer just parents and kids or neighbors or relatives figuring out how to spend their time. These new actors have financial profit as their goal, and are not necessarily bound to the larger purposes of the original human activities when they occur outside the cash economy. Investors in health care systems are looking for profit, not health care. Commercial theme park developers are interested in making money; kids enjoying themselves is just a secondary by-product. Video game promoters are interested in customers with spending money, not children with interests.

Thus, there is tremendous competition for access to our children and youth as consumers. James McNeal, author of *The Kids Market: Myths and Realities,* is one of the leading experts on selling to children. Writing in *Mothering Magazine,* Gary Ruskin reports that McNeal sees children as economic resources to be mined. To show just how despicable this can be, he cites the work of Cheryl Idell, a consultant who has written about advertising strategy for corporate clients seeking to sell to children. According to Ruskin's report, Idell advocates that corporate clients capitalize upon nagging and whining by children to motivate parents to make purchases. "In other words, Idell's job is to make your life miserable." This is business as usual in much of corporate America, and why some psychologists have asked the American Psychological Association to declare collaboration with this process a violation of ethical standards.

Of course, it is sometimes possible for commercial enterprises to do good and do well, but doing good is secondary to financial accounting. It must be, or the systems built on the prevailing economic concepts go bankrupt. An economy not dominated by the dollar is not necessarily more altruistic, but it does accept a much wider range of currencies: love, duty, religious belief, political ideology, barter, and good old-fashioned neighborliness.

We offer one important caveat: In many technologically primitive societies, meeting basic needs in a nonmonetarized economy takes up most of the people's time and often involves backbreaking and soul-deadening labor. In Sudan, we met rural women who spent eight hours each day getting water and wood for cooking. They had long walks to and from the stream and the woodpile. Imagine how rich they felt when an international development agency installed a well with a hand-operated pump in their village and showed them how to make energy-efficient stoves that cut their fuel use in half! Hours and hours of time were freed up for other activities.

However, in our technologically modern societies many of us are becoming as time-poor as those rural Sudanese women were initially. For us, the challenges come from the time-consuming activities associated with working in a cash-driven economy. Commuting to work, for example, costs a lot of time—*hours* per day are not unusual in some places (urban and rural) and for some workers.

Where Do Children and Families Stand in the Two Economies?

If we look at the whole family, rather than just any one individual, some clear themes have emerged over the past forty to fifty years. Middle- and working-class families now are much more time-poor than they once were. When most families had an adult at home during the week, most took care of business during the workweek. They earned their money 9 to 5, Monday to Friday. They cleaned, shopped, cooked, made dentist and doctor appointments, had repairmen in, and all the other aspects of running a household at that same time. Most stores and services were closed evenings and Sundays, and perhaps open a half day on Saturdays. As a result, *families* were time-rich. Evenings and weekends were free.

In 1960, more than 60 percent of families with middle-class incomes had one parent who supported the family primarily inside the cash economy while the other worked outside it, in the nonmonetarized economy. By 1990, that figure had dropped to less than 25 percent, and it continues to decline. Further, the proportion of families with two adults has decreased also—from about 90 percent in 1960 to less than 70 percent by the mid-1990s—which means that one person is probably trying to do two full-time jobs, one inside the cash economy and outside, as a parent and partner. Most of them are time-poor.

In addition to being time-poor, we have become more aware of the costs of choosing where we spend our time, what economists call "opportunity costs." An opportunity cost arises when alternative uses of time compete, when doing A means not doing B, and when one of the two generates cash. If your son or daughter has a ball game Thursday night and your boss wants you to work that evening, you must choose. Attending the game costs the amount you would earn for those hours at work. Staying home to care for a young child costs you the salary you forgo by doing so. Of course, opportunity costs increase as the market value of your time increases. It is a complicated chain of connection, but an important one. It costs a person earning $50 per hour twice as much in opportunity costs to attend a Little League game as it does someone earning $25 per hour and five times as much as it does a person earning $10 per hour (although the percentages of time and income remain the same).

With women on average now earning much less than men—about 70 percent—it's pretty clear that if we think only about the financial costs and benefits, then most families will end up with women spending more time with children than men—staying home with infants and sick children, working part-time to accommodate school schedules, and attending parent-teacher conferences. This remains true even after the massive increase in mothers working in the cash economy over the last forty years. In 1950, 22 percent of women with children were in the paid labor force (19 percent of those with preschoolers and 33 percent of those with older children). By 1990 that figure had risen to 67 percent overall (and 58 percent of mothers with preschoolers). In the year 2000 it is even higher.

Who is paying for this shift in the economic roles of mothers? Some fathers are stepping up their involvement, and some community institutions are increasing their efforts to help families adjust—for example, through after-school programs. But the data tell us that most fathers have not changed much. Mothers, in contrast, have typically made heroic efforts to keep up their productive activities in human capital investment while stepping into the dollar-driven labor force. But there are limits to what even a mother can do or wants to do.

Earning more money is always tempting, partly because it is easy to miss the price of those added earnings in terms of time and energy that could be devoted to other activities. Sometimes, it is more than just not appreciating the social and psychological costs, but of expecting someone else to incur them. That leads us to the concept of *externalized costs*.

Living in the Land of Opportunity Costs

Economists use the term *externalizing* to refer to the process of shifting costs onto someone beyond the scope of your responsibility. For example, suppose a factory is producing a ton of sludge each day as a by-product of its manufacturing process. Safely processing and disposing of that sludge is costly, perhaps $2,500 per day. But dumping the sludge into a nearby river is cheap from the factory owner's perspective.

Of course, the people who live downriver pay the price of coping with polluted water, but from the factory owner's point of view that's their problem. The factory owner has externalized the waste-control costs. Obviously, the more you can externalize costs, the higher your profits will be, so long as the community you depend on for employees, markets, and services continues to function despite the costs you are passing along to it.

What are the incentives for internalizing costs? Bad publicity is one; a local news program might editorialize about the pollution. Moral scruples are another; the factory owner might be troubled by the ethical violations. Public regulation is a third; government might move in to regulate waste disposal. Each has its place. But the impulse to externalize remains strong nonetheless.

How does the concept of externalizing costs apply to families? For one thing, when employers do not assume responsibility for the physical and psychological effects of the workplace on employees, they are externalizing those costs. When families don't meet their responsibilities to care for their children, they are passing along those costs—externalizing them—to the larger community. The result? Serious threats to the community's human capital. Delinquency and dropout rates may go up. More teenage girls may get pregnant and become unwed mothers. This is one way to frame the issue of parental responsibility that we wrestled with earlier in this book.

When we analyze human capital costs and benefits, we can do so from the viewpoint of the individual, the family, or the community—and come up with different costs and benefits for the same choices. For example, adolescents love to make money, but on average, teenagers who work in the cash economy twenty or more hours a week seem to suffer substantial costs: their grades are lower, their investment in pro-social activities decreases, their experimentation with drugs, alcohol, and sex increases. That's costly for the community, even though it puts more money in teenagers' pockets and increases the GNP.

Of course, some families depend upon teenagers' income to make ends meet, and others find that for their teenagers, the kind of work they do actually contributes to their character development. What adolescents choose to do with their earnings also has varying costs and benefits. If they use their money for immediate spending, they support the large consumer market that has grown up around teenagers' income. If they save it for college or some other future activity that will develop their abilities, they will make society more productive and satisfying. Their choice may also relate to their self-esteem: Do they come to value themselves as consumers or as producers?

When both parents leave home for outside work, families may increase their cash income but pay a substantial price in the domestic sphere and feel stressed and guilty about that. At the same time, the community may be called upon to pick up the costs of child care. As the process of transferring life from the parallel economy into the cash economy proceeds, opportunity costs and the impulse to shift costs to someone else rise proportionately.

Remember, you can't calculate opportunity costs unless someone is offering to pay for your time. How do people decide if they are willing to pay those costs? One factor is how they view society's values. If you face opportunity costs, paying them may seem less attractive if your society denigrates the goods and services of a nonmonetarized economy. In a society like ours, where the cash economy is voraciously dominant, are the best things in life still free? No. They are very costly—be the price directly financial (as in the case of paying admission to the pool) or indirectly financial (as in income lost through taking time off to smell the roses).

Children thrive when adults *invest* time in them and when adults *spend* time with them. Both are important. There is trouble ahead when we as parents are not willing to pay the opportunity costs of family activities and instead externalize them to someone beyond the family. The results can affect schooling, family life, and community institutions. Teachers today are nearly unanimous in believing that parents expect the schools to do some of the basic socialization and care-giving for kids that used to take place at home—for example, sex education and character development. They don't say, "Parents are externalizing the costs of child rearing," but that's precisely what they mean.

Whether intended or not, the result is a growing unwillingness in our society to subsidize childhood as a time of freedom—free play, free feeling, free ride. This is evident in the increasing financial problems our schools face. Tightening budgets put pressure first and foremost upon the key socializing aspects of education: extracurricular activities like clubs and sports, meal programs, and the arts. All this is misguided policy because it narrowly looks at the monetarized economy of child rearing and loses sight of the vast value added to the community's human capital by these activities.

How Can Parents Teach Children to Be Mindful About the Economic Life?

The drive to greater and ever-earlier payoffs increases the pressure on children to perform, to mature, and to succeed in ways that lend prestige to parents; the way children respond is by upping their demands as consumers. For example, for many families, success in school is of unprecedented importance. In the 1950s, a high school degree was an acceptable goal even for middle-class kids, and there was no powerful stigma attached to dropping out before graduation for blue-collar kids. Now the expectations for educational attainment are much higher. Parents fear that their children will be shut out of the economy and react by stepping up their efforts to obtain a competitive advantage.

Parents and educators raise their academic expectations for young children in anticipation of future competition. Where learning to read was once a goal in the early grades, some teachers and parents now want children to be reading as they enter first grade, and often express concern for children who are not reading fluently by winter break. These children are considered delayed, even learning-disabled. Secondary school graduation has come to be defined as a prerequisite for functioning as a normal person in our society. A college education is seen as imperative for families across the social and economic spectrum. All this means that children are under greater pressure to pay off in academic skills than ever before. In this climate, free play may seem a luxury children cannot afford if they are to be successful, even though there are good reasons to believe that free play is a good investment for later success in the form of improved motor and social skills.

In a nation where everything costs money and continues to cost more, most families need two incomes to keep up, although because of divorce and single parenthood, more and more families have only one potential wage earner. Most families used to have a buffer. If a child got sick, someone could be home. If the principal wage earner was laid off, the other adult could find a job to compensate. By holding one adult in reserve, families could spread themselves more evenly over both economies. They didn't have all their eggs in one basket.

Now they do. Either they need two cash incomes to meet their commitments in the cash economy, or there is only one adult in the household, with no backup.

We can teach our children to be mindful about the visible and invisible costs that accompany every human activity. First, we need to understand the value of time, and then help our children understand it as well. What do any of us really have, after all is said and done? We have our time on this earth (and whatever else our religious beliefs tell us may come before or after). We have what some spiritual teachers call "the present moment." When it comes to everything else, we are all just renting (or perhaps leasing). No one owns. We spend our time. We invest our time. We waste our time. The clock ticks.

What we do with our time—each present moment—is the single most important indicator of our values and beliefs about the world. We spend our time in all kinds of ways and must decide if we are spending it wisely or foolishly. Are we investing or wasting? When we spend time preparing for some future goal, we are investing time with the expectation of payoff. The one thing we can't really do with time is save it; each moment passes and can never be recovered (except perhaps in memory). This must be the starting point for understanding mindful parenting in a material world.

"Money makes the world go around." So sings a character in the Broadway musical *Cabaret.* In a financially driven society like ours, one of the biggest challenges parents face is teaching children to be mindful about money. The social environment makes this particularly difficult because we are bombarded with messages that push us in the opposite direction—monetary mindlessness. How can we teach our children monetary mindfulness amid all these undermining messages?

We find guidance for parents on this matter in what might at first blush seem an unlikely source, a best-selling book on the lifestyle of the rich entitled *The Millionaire Next Door,* by business professors Thomas Stanley and William Danko. Their book is a fascinating exploration of how people accumulate wealth and what they do with it. Rather than glorifying the worst of the materialist economy of spend, spend, spend, however, the authors' research offers insight into monetary mindfulness. They conclude that most people who become rich (assets exceeding a million dollars) and enable their offspring to get rich too, do so by following a set of guidelines that represent mindfulness (although neither the authors nor the people they interviewed were likely to put it in those terms).

To start with, they embrace one of the most important principles of alternative economics, namely that wealth and income are very different states of being. Benjamin Franklin offered the maxim that a man who spends one penny more than he earns is poor, while a man who spends one penny less than he earns is rich. That is going a bit too far, of course, yet there is an important truth in Franklin's aphorism. The key to wealth is accumulating assets so that you can become free of the rat race to earn more that comes when you gear your spending to your income (rather than trying to meet needs with as little spending as possible).

Stanley and Danko cite numerous examples and provide extensive statistical data to show that the relationship between income and wealth is not as direct as many people assume. Many families with relatively high incomes have little or no accumulated wealth, and conversely, many families with quite modest incomes have substantial wealth. Who succeeds in accumulating wealth? By and large, families that are frugal, pay attention to savings, and don't spend just to "keep up with the Joneses." In short, families that practice financial mindfulness. Naturally, there are exceptions, individuals who inherit enormous wealth and hold on to it, or strike it rich through some unusual talent or by seizing a unique money-making opportunity—rock stars, movie stars, Internet stars, and the like. But these folks are the exceptions.

Accumulating wealth is in itself a major accomplishment, of course. But of equal or even greater import are families who succeed in transmitting their successful behaviors, values, and attributes to their children. Stanley and Danko provide some insight into why some parents succeed in this task while others fail. Indeed, many children of rich parents become financially inept and become addicted to spending. The net result is that they either move dramatically downward economically or retain their status only through heavy subsidies from their parents.

Not surprisingly, temperament plays a role. Some kids are easier to teach financial mindfulness to than others. What is

184

more, parents often inadvertently create financial monsters by trying to make the lives of their children easier. Their impulse is understandable, but here, as elsewhere, easier in the short run may mean harder in the long run. Stanley and Danko offer ten "Rules for Affluent Parents and Productive Children," and they are worth our time. Their book tells the whole story; here we will simply summarize.

1. *Never tell children that their parents are wealthy.* If children's social maps include the element "We are rich," kids may seek to live like rich people rather than to become productive.

2. *No matter how wealthy you are, teach your children discipline and frugality.* Doing this by example is naturally the most effective strategy. "Spend as I do," is a good and effective motto if parents demonstrate monetary mindfulness. One affluent father we know made a point of collecting his loose change and periodically bringing it to the bank for paper money. It was a twice-a-year family ritual that sent the message that every penny matters.

3. *Assure that your children won't realize you're affluent until they have established a mature, disciplined, and adult lifestyle and profession.* One way the authors (and the affluent parents they studied) recommend is to avoid giving cash gifts to kids. Ironically, the more their kids appear to need these gifts, the more unwise it is to give them.

4. *Minimize discussions about the items that each child and grandchild will inherit or receive as gifts.* This shifts attention away from the present toward some future expectation of bounty, and that undermines motivation to become a productive person and misdirects family feelings away from relationships toward material values.

185

5. *Never give cash or other significant gifts to your adult children as part of a negotiation strategy.* As the authors put it, "Give because of love, even obligation and kindness." Trying to buy kids off or bribe them is never a good idea. In fact, it is not a good idea at *any* age.

6. *Stay out of your adult children's family matters.* The definition of adulthood is the ability to take responsibility for self and others. Parents can start early, whenever morally possible, by letting kids experience the natural consequences of their actions (so long as those consequences are not permanently damaging).

7. *Don't try to compete with your children.* This is one reason why the children of affluent parents face some big challenges. The more parents show off their wealth, the more discouraged their children become about their ability to meet their parents' standards.

8. *Always remember that your children are individuals.* Parental efforts to balance out differences among siblings by giving more to one child than another rarely work, and generally just increase resentment and sibling rivalry.

9. *Emphasize your children's achievements, no matter how small, not their or your symbols of success.* As the authors put it, "Teach your children to achieve, not just to consume." Kids need authentic foundations for being proud of themselves if they are to feel self-esteem. No child can truly believe he or she is great if the only sign of it is the cost of what their parents can buy them to wear or drive. Such accoutrements can actually undermine self-worth by emphasizing the child's weakness, vulnerability, and dependence, since no child can compete with the material power of an affluent parent. Add to that the intrinsic emptiness of material possessions when stacked up against character and spiritual

development, and it is clear that this is a self-defeating strategy.

10. *Tell your children that there are a lot of things more valuable than money.* Showing them would be still better. Interesting advice to result from an analysis of rich families. Those who respond, "That's easy for you to say, since you are rich!" would miss the point. It is a message deeply grounded in reality.

The one area in which most of the rich agree that it does make sense to invest large amounts of money in their children is education and professional development. Rich families regard putting money into education as not spending but rather investment, a lesson everyone should learn, including parents and policy makers.

These guidelines are useful for most families in our society, regardless of their income. Why? Because by global standards most families in our society *are* rich. When the poverty line in India is defined as a diet of less than 2,000 calories per day and the average annual family income for much of the world is measured in hundreds of dollars, American families are affluent. This is the global reality behind the poverty that plagues American families with incomes below $20,000 per year for a family of four. The point is that every child can benefit from monetary mindfulness, and every family can learn something from the guidelines that the richest Americans follow to preserve wealth and protect their children from being spoiled. Once we understand that message, we are ready to take stock of our daily lives. Joe Dominguez and Vicki Robin's classic book *Your Money or Your Life* shows how.

Conclusion

This chapter explored the pressures imposed on parents when society shifts to an economy dominated by the dollar value of everything, with all that this implies for the "commercialization" of childhood. Advertising and marketing aimed at children create impossible demands on parents, no matter what their income level, and sow the seeds of later mindless spending and superficial materialism in children that can poison their character development. Finding ways to live more fully outside the monetarized economy while reaping its benefits and participating effectively inside it is a struggle, but an attainable goal if parents live and teach mindfulness.

Lesson: Wealth comes not from giving in to the commercial "pusher" who promises satisfaction through material acquisition, but only through mindful living, no matter what your income, and from a sense of personal connection to life's enduring values: love, the investment of energy, wisdom, joy, and affirmation.

9

Mastering Television, Video Games, and the Internet

The Influence of TV: Compared with What?

Without some basis for comparison, it is extremely difficult—nearly impossible, in fact—for any of us to analyze and
understand that which is around us all the time. This is part of
the message in the lines quoted in Chapter 3 from the German
poet and philosopher Goethe: "What is the most difficult of
all? . . . To see with one's eyes what is lying before them." This
is what we face when we try to understand the roles that television, video games, and the Internet play in the life of children
and youth in the twenty-first century.

The Internet is new enough for many of us to be aware of life
B.T.I.—before the Internet. We can recall the time before we
were on-line. Jim can easily recall his first office fax machine,

in 1986. He remembers pondering with his colleagues whether or not the Erikson Institute should purchase one, or simply bring the occasional to-be-faxed letter downstairs to the office-supply store that would send out and receive faxes for a flat fee per page. Within weeks the fax had become standard equipment in the office, and the staff could hardly imagine how they had done without it. Claire actually had one in her home office by 1989.

And the Internet? Jim logged on with his first e-mail address in 1994, and Claire by 1996. Now we are just two of many millions in the United States and tens of millions around the world. According to the most recent estimates, by the year 2000 most Americans had Internet access (if not at home, then through some public facility like a library). Even our parents are on-line now! But it is all new enough, and there are still so many people who are not connected, that meaningful comparisons can be made between the "ons" and the "offs."

But what about television? When we ask, "What effect does television have?" the first clarifying question is, "Compared with what?" For a basis for comparison, we need to go back half a century, when television was first entering our lives. Concern about the possible effects of television viewing began with the earliest introduction of broadcast and reception facilities in the late 1930s and early 1940s, before its widespread dissemination was put on hold with the outbreak of World War II. As early as 1936, a British social psychologist named T. H. Pear raised the question when he wrote, "What differences will television make to our habits and mental attitudes?" We are still trying to figure that out.

Looking back more than half a century later, we can see that most of the effort devoted to answering Pear's question systematically has been geared to assessing the effect of television in transmitting and stimulating aggression in children. By 1972, a report to the U.S. Surgeon General, entitled *Television and Growing Up: The Impact of Televised Violence*, looked at hundreds of research reports and focused almost exclusively on this topic. By the 1990s the American Psychological Association was looking at thousands of studies and concluded that there was a direct link between viewing violence on television and increased aggression by children and youth. The American Academy of Pediatrics has joined the psychologists in warning of these effects.

By now it seems clear to most unbiased observers that televised violence increases aggressive behavior. How big is the effect? The American Psychological Association's report concluded that by itself TV violence accounts for about 10 percent of the variation in children's aggressive behavior. Our calculator for risk and opportunity shows us that rarely is a single cause primarily responsible for any particular outcome in children. Television is no exception.

Ten percent. Is that a big or a small effect? In the real world, that's a big effect, when something so important as aggression by children is at stake, about as big as the effect of smoking on cancer. Most people who smoke don't get cancer, but even most addicted smokers now realize that smoking increases cancer risk significantly, and this knowledge is the basis for a massive antismoking public health campaign. There are laws governing when and where adults may smoke and a ban on cigarette sales to kids. Yet we have few restrictions on television; how many people even consider TV a public health issue?

And what about TV's other influences on children (and parents)? How does television viewing by both child and parent affect parent-child interaction? How does it affect the vitally important processes of peer interaction? Does parents' using television as a baby-sitter affect their kids' development, particularly in temperamentally challenging children? And, how does the child's free and largely unregulated access to television affect other activities? Big, tough questions, to be sure, but questions that demand answers.

Interestingly, some of the research needed to address these questions was done in the 1950s, when American life was just starting to reorganize itself around the television set. Researchers in the late 1940s and early 1950s asked parents why they were buying their first television set. "To bring the family together in the home" was the most common response.

With the 20/20 hindsight of half a century's experience, that seems an ironic response, because when researchers examined what introducing a TV set to a family meant in terms of its time together, they found something rather disturbing. Developmental psychologist Eleanor Maccoby reported in 1951 that 78 percent of the families said no conversation occurred during viewing except during commercials. Maccoby described what television meant to family life this way in her 1951 report: "The television atmosphere in most households is one of quiet absorption on the part of the family members who are present as 'parallel' rather than interactive, and the set does seem quite clearly to dominate family life when it is on" (p. 428). Sounds familiar, doesn't it?

A study conducted in 1956 found that for 36 percent of the families, watching TV was the only activity everyone participated in during the week. It also found that watching television was substituting for other social activities within the family, and outside it in the community. Sound familiar?

One of the earliest findings about children and television was that parents didn't know how much television their children were watching. That remains true today. Early on, researchers found that children were exercising heavy influence in the choice of what to watch. What is more, by 1969 more than 25 percent of households in the United States contained two or more TV sets. Today most households do.

What about the crucial issue of how television affected the relations between children and their parents? Eleanor Maccoby asked mothers this question: "Has TV made it easier or harder to take care of the children at home?" Fifty-four percent replied "easier," 33 percent replied "no difference," and only 3 percent said it made it harder. Why?

Maccoby reported that mothers told her "It's much easier—it's like putting him to sleep." And she concluded, "Mothers comment that TV keeps the children much quieter—there is less roughhousing and less bothering the parents with questions" (p. 440). Other studies found that in response to the statement "TV keeps the children quiet," 62 percent of parents replied "Strongly agree," 26 percent said "Agree," and only 12 percent said they disagreed. Perhaps when President Richard Nixon spoke of the "silent majority" in 1969, he was on to something.

Why is the effect of television on family interaction so important? Because children need the experience of working things out with parents and other adults, how to manage complex social relationships. Child rearing cannot be accomplished via remote control, especially with temperamentally challenging children. We can readily imagine that in the pre-TV parenting era parents had no choice but to work with and work on these challenging children to find some basis for teaching them to get along effectively. There was no choice. There was nowhere else to go. Now parents could postpone dealing with difficult children by sitting them down in front of the television. "It's like putting them to sleep," parents told Eleanor Maccoby in 1950. But this short-term solution only made the problem worse in the long run.

And it had reverberations throughout the world of children. For one thing, children's standards for interaction changed. Few live teachers can compete with the "production values" of television. As TV became more and more visually sophisticated, this gap grew. By the late 1970s, college students were prone to treat live classroom lectures as if they were TV programs—both expecting to be entertained and forgetting that what they did as "an audience" mattered to "the program" (the professor).

These changes have crept up on us over the decades. Now, as parents feel themselves to be under siege, there is ever greater willingness to ask again the question T. H. Pear asked in 1936, only now in the past tense. What differences *did* television make to our habits and mental attitudes?

As television and movies have become more visually explicit in their treatment of violence and horror, another issue is trauma. Trauma is the simultaneous experience of being overpowered by unmanageable negative feelings and having your vision of the world blown away by horror. With the power of contemporary special effects coupled with the no-holds-barred approach to subject matter, it is little wonder that the potentially traumatic impact of television and the movies is now an issue as never before. In her 1998 book *Mommy, I'm Scared: How TV and Movies Frighten Children and What We Can Do to Protect Them,* psychologist Joanne Cantor offered some very disturbing early research on this issue.

In her study, adolescents and young adults were asked to recall fright reactions to the mass media, including the news. About 90 percent recalled such reactions. More than 25 percent reported that the reaction had lasted at least a year. More than half reported reactions that included difficulty in sleeping or eating. More than 20 percent reported "subsequent mental preoccupation with the frightening aspects of the stimulus." Movies like *Jaws* (sharks) and *Halloween* (mass murder) were associated with the most severe symptoms. The findings of traumatic impact were validated by other studies, including one that asked parents to identify their children's responses and found that the reports of children and parents coincided in documenting traumatic responses.

Today, conflicts over television watching and concerns about its effects on kids are on our minds, and lead many parents to believe that the overall effect of television is to make children more challenging to handle than ever before. Parents today often resent TV's influence on their children—even if only vaguely and with a sense of fatalism about the possibilities for change. They worry that television is making their children more aggressive, more materialistic, and more obnoxious. Most parents laugh and shake their heads when told that only 3 percent of their predecessors in Maccoby's 1950s research thought television made child rearing harder. Parents today worry about the influence of TV on their children. They should. But, what's next?

What Can Parents Do About It?

Doing something about television is an uphill battle. The radical solution chosen by some families is simply to turn it off, perhaps expelling the television from their home. One father we know put it this way:

> I grew up watching TV. I love TV! But when our son was born, I knew that if the television stayed in our house it would take its toll on my relationship with Jason. I knew myself well enough to know that it could distract me from him. And I was sure it would hook him too. I knew that in today's society it would rob him of so many beautiful and creative ways to use his time better. And then there's the violence. That's not what I wanted for him or for me so the TV had to go. Maybe later, when he's older, I'll bring it back into the house. Maybe.

That is certainly one way to change the family dynamic, and for some families it may be the only way. The American Academy of Pediatrics recommends children not watch any television for the first four years of life. In her books *The Plug-in*

Drug and *Unplugging the Plug-in Drug,* social critic Marie Winn reports on how this process works and how it affects family dynamics. She finds it a tough but a rewarding effort. Schools can help, as Stanford University researcher Tom Robinson found when he demonstrated that a school-based program for elementary age kids could reduce TV watching and thus reduce aggressive behavior six months later.

But abstinence is so far from the day-to-day experience of most families that it seems unlikely to catch on as a common approach. Most of us like to watch television. Some of what is available is wonderful. So, if not total abstinence, what then? Two good resources in figuring out a family strategy for television are Nancy Carlsson-Paige and Diane Levin's *Who's Calling the Shots?* (particularly for families with young children) and Dave Grossman and Gloria DeGaetano's *Stop Teaching Our Kids to Kill* (particularly for families with older children and teenagers).

Both sets of authors remind parents that there is more to this issue than simply the private actions and concerns of adults and children in families. There are social policy issues here that make a difference for families. Until the early 1990s broadcasters were required to work within the limits and guidelines provided by the Act for Children's Television, federal legislation that required TV stations to justify their children's broadcasting on the basis of how it served positive educational and developmental goals. Today we have the V-chip—a technology that promises to permit parents to block out certain television material. But will it work? Some say no, because kids may find ways to thwart it, the most vulnerable kids will not be protected because their parents can't or won't invest in it, and because the producers of TV programs will find ways to avoid it.

When the legislation regulating children's television ended, things changed. As Carlsson-Paige and Levin point out, the major networks immediately fired their children's television staffs and replaced them with new people with marketing and advertising backgrounds. Today children's television has become a more blatantly merchandizing medium than ever before. And this does not even begin to consider the ongoing problem with violent images, the more general problem of how television viewing affects the social experience of children and parents, and the broader problem of cultural degradation.

Two dramatic examples are worth mentioning, one from abroad and one closer to home. From 1964 to 1994, the number of American children who were obese increased from 5 percent to 13 percent. Research conducted at Stanford University reports that when kids participate in a program to reduce television watching, their weight goes down. Thus, we know that watching television is linked to obesity. How does this play out in particularly vulnerable populations?

In the South Pacific, reports from Polynesia indicate how the introduction of television has had an insidious effect. In a culture in which eating disorders were virtually unknown, bulimia and anorexia have become increasingly common. For reasons of diet and genetics, Polynesian girls tend to be quite heavy by the standard American images of femininity.

If the wraithlike Calista Flockhart of Ally McBeal stands at one end of the spectrum of body types, the typical Polynesian girl stands at the other. As Polynesian girls have been exposed to American TV, they have developed rampant dissatisfaction with how they look and have resorted to dangerous dieting. A 1999 report indicates alarming rates of bulimia and anorexia.

According to psychologist Mary Pipher, American girls are not immune. In her book *Reviving Ophelia,* Pipher reveals how the physical standards of feminine beauty in the mass media have become ever more unrealistic and unattainable in recent decades. During the same period, the bombardment of ever more intense and explicit sexual messages has heightened the pressure on young women. One of Pipher's examples is particularly telling: The Miss Swedens of the 1950s were two inches shorter and forty pounds heavier than today's beauty queens. At a time when obesity has increased 25 percent among American kids over the last thirty years, this means fewer and fewer girls can hope to meet such unrealistic standards. The result is stress, worry, and excessive dieting.

The story of television is still unfolding. With the advent of cable and the VCR, kids are being exposed to unprecedented varieties of images and influences. Concerns abound, whether it is violently explicit wrestling and sexually explicit romance, or the effects of reduced interaction at home. Our ecological perspective reminds us to regard these influences in the larger context of social toxicity and the accumulation of risk in the lives of our children and youth. That's a sobering thought, but one that need not defeat us. We can gain control over TV viewing, and we can teach children to process what they see with a more critical eye. Now that we know the potential costs and effects of television, we can do a better job of countering them with developmental assets, mindfulness, and higher consciousness.

The Internet

It has been five decades since television came to dominate American homes, and the issues it raised in the 1950s remain. But today many of those issues have become obscured because there is little basis for comparison. The people who do not watch television or who do not own one are such a small and unusual minority, it is difficult to compare them to everyone else. This point is worth remembering when we move on to consider the Internet, where a basis for comparison (before and after) is still available—at least for a while.

The Internet is in many ways "television squared." It offers the individual child or youth amazing access to the world, access that adults are hard pressed to manage. Each year the possibilities increase dramatically. While most of the attention now focuses on commercial and educational possibilities, anyone concerned with the well-being of children requires a more complete understanding. And to do that we must repeat all the questions that were raised—but never fully answered—about television: How does the Internet affect social interaction? How does it affect parents' authority in the lives of their children? How does it facilitate access to the dark side of life? What kind of culture does it present, amplify, and endorse?

As always, the best answer is, "It depends." Some data are worrisome. For example, a study conducted at Carnegie Mellon University tracked the impact of Internet access over a two-year period (among adults). The researchers found that the more people logged on to the Internet, the worse their communications with family members, the smaller their social network, and the more depressed and lonely they felt.

That finding makes a lot of sense to us. At a time when we need to pay more attention to being fully present, the Internet can make us more distant and disconnected. The analogies to television are striking. A study conducted in Canada in the early 1960s tracked the impact of television's beginning to broadcast in one community and found that within six months there was a 25 percent reduction of face-to-face interaction among its residents.

Another concern about the Internet is that it allows children and youth direct access to the dark side of life and our culture. Although enforcement is weak, we have some standards of decency and developmental appropriateness when it comes to children's access to sex and violence in movie theaters. R and X rated movies are at least officially off limits to kids. There are some restrictions on television programs also, although the rise of cable TV has weakened these barriers substantially. But the

Internet offers easy and direct access to the most vile and degrading images and narratives imaginable (and beyond what most people can imagine). A mother checks up on her young son's computer and finds he has been visiting and downloading hard core pornography with an ease and a casualness that appalls her.

What is more, some of the most vulgar Web sites kids can visit are deliberately misleading—for instance, search for the White House for a social studies project, and you may end up at Whitehouse.com, an XX rated porno site (Whitehouse.org being the president's address). Some porno sites lure Web surfers by using an Internet address (a URL) only slightly different from popular regular sites—from ESPN.com the sports site to EPSM.com the sadomasochist site. Do our culture and young people really need more and easier exposure to degrading vulgarity? We don't think so.

In addition to degradation, there is the issue of validation for antisocial behavior and alienation. Thirty years ago, if you were the most alienated kid on your block, perhaps a boy filled with rage at the injustice of life and steeped in a sense of meaninglessness, you would have had a hard time finding other kids like yourself. As a result, there was a pull back to the mainstream, the normalizing influence of social support. But now? Today you can log on to any number of Web sites and chat rooms and find validation for your alienation, your rage, and your antisocial fantasies. How about logging on to alienation.com? It's a real site we visited in an effort to see just how bad things are. They are that bad.

In the year before the Columbine High School shootings, Eric Harris was posting florid hate messages on the Internet through a chat room. One family did copy them and report them to the local police, but only because of the direct threat to their son. As is well known by now, the police apparently did nothing with the complaint. But that is not our concern. We are concerned that in the world of chat rooms anything goes. Some are vile, vulgar, and outrageous in their flamboyant rhetoric of alienation and rage, where what Eric wrote is commonplace. That is business as usual on the dark side of the culture.

Shortly after the Columbine shootings, *New York Times* journalist Amy Harmon reported on the on-line response to what Eric and Dylan did. Her conclusion: "In on-line discussions, on World Wide Web sites and in E-mail, young people are engaging in what amounts to a fragmented national dialogue over social ostracism and the unforgiving hierarchies of adolescent life. . . . Almost all of the electronic empathizers were quick to repudiate the killings. But many wrote of identifying with the harassment." One respondent wrote that he "proudly supports the trench coat mafia." Two years later a 19-year-old in California plotted to blow up his community college, and advertised both his rage and his admiration for Eric Harris and Dylan Klebold on his own vile Web site.

The dark side of the Internet magnifies, validates, and extends the dark side of the culture as it is shaped in music (from the absolute nihilism of rocker Marilyn Manson to the foul and hateful lyrics of some gangsta rap music), in movies and television (where the boundaries of the cruel and vicious seem to expand each year), and in video games, where all the nastiness comes together in a coherent whole. But with video games there is more than imagery. There is practice in the arts of violence.

Video Games

In World War II, when regular American soldiers went into combat, less than 20 percent could shoot their rifles at the enemy. Why? They had learned to shoot at targets, a skill that does not transfer automatically to shooting people. Why? For the most part, human beings have an inhibition against killing. We must be trained to remove this inhibition, trained to kill.

This is the conclusion reached by military psychologist Dave Grossman in his book *On Killing: The Psychological Cost of Learning to Kill in War and Society.*

Today, more than 90 percent of first-time soldiers can shoot at the enemy. Why? Training procedures have changed. Soldiers practice shooting at human forms, and that training breaks down the resistance against killing. What is the most effective and efficient tool for such training? The same point-and-shoot video games available to kids in almost every mall and movie theater lobby in the country, and in many homes as well.

And it isn't just shooting. The following analysis of a video game appeared in TRANSFER, an Internet newsletter on transit and urban development issues. "A new computer game by Aspyr Media awards points to players for their speed, racing style, and for hitting pedestrians. The game, Carmageddon, challenges its virtual drivers to 'race alone or over friends' and mocks: 'Pedestrians don't *always* have the right of way.'" A British study observed fifty boys playing a nonviolent video game and another fifty boys randomly selected to watch a martial arts game. Then both groups were shown a series of ambiguous photographs. When asked to interpret them, the kids who had played the violent game "interpreted" the photos in a more hostile way. Playing violent videos had contaminated the kids' consciousness. This parallels findings about television: adults who watch a lot of television tend to become more paranoid, suspicious, and distrustful of society.

Violent video games are popular, particularly with boys. One study found that 50 percent of the boys surveyed named violent video games as their favorites. What is more, increasing numbers of young men are developing the technical knowledge to customize their violent games—as did Eric Harris in Littleton. And their interest in violent video games often compounds as they play.

Paul Lynch and his colleagues have found that violent video games produced stronger physiological changes than nonviolent games. These included elevated heart rate and blood pressure, as well as aggression-related hormones, adrenaline and testosterone. These effects were greatest for the boys who were most angry and hostile before playing the games.

Craig Anderson and Karen Dill confirmed these findings when they tested the level of aggressive thoughts and behavior for two groups of boys. The first was randomly selected to play a technically challenging nonviolent video game; the second to play an equally challenging violent game. The boys randomly selected to play the violent game showed more aggressive thoughts and behavior than the other boys. The title of Grossman and DeGaetano's book sends exactly the right message: *Stop Teaching Our Kids to Kill.* As more and more community leaders awake to the danger, they are beginning to act. Each week brings more efforts to regulate access to the point-and-shoot video games that pose such a psychological danger. In July 2000, Indianapolis, Indiana, adopted what was thought to be the first law to make the most violent games off-limits to kids. David Grossman tracks the progress of these efforts and interested parties can participate in the movement through his electronic messaging (e-mail at LtColDaveG@aol.com).

Conclusion

The effect of televised violence on the aggressive behavior of children is about as strong as the effect of smoking on cancer. With media images of violence everywhere, how do parents protect their children? With the advent of the Internet, the challenge of monitoring the quality of a child's experience with the dark side of our culture increases. Add point-and-shoot video games to the equation, and the challenge grows to dangerous proportions. As always, it is the most psychologically vulnerable kids who are most likely to be pushed over the edge by these socially toxic influences. In West Paducah, Kentucky, 14-year-old Michael Carneal became so proficient at his point-and-shoot video game that after he practiced only one afternoon with a stolen pistol, the troubled boy walked into his school and hit every one of his targets: eight teenagers attending a prayer group meeting.

What can parents do? Individually, they can take steps to limit exposure in their own homes—monitor computer use, limit TV viewing, keep the point-and-shoot video games out of the home. It's not easy. We know that as parents. That's why it's not enough to act as an individual parent. We must also work together as citizens to make the world a safer place for kids. But as always, we must start with ourselves, and then we can act with confidence and insight.

Lesson: To find a place of peace amid the noise of our addiction to media stimulation is impossible unless we first visit the deepest, calmest place to be found in human experience, namely the inner life of meditation, and then use this mindfulness to lead our children away from the dark side of the culture.

Epilogue: Being a Good Parent and a Good Citizen

&o Parents are under siege, but with access to the right tools they can find their way through the maze of emotions, social pressures, and dilemmas they face in raising their children. We remain hopeful that through mindfulness, spiritual connection, and social activism parents can lift the siege.

One important element of this effort lies in the realm of what is ordinarily called values, but which is perhaps better termed virtues and character. There is increasing recognition throughout our society that not enough attention is paid to this topic, and that more and more kids are looking to peers for their values. Thus, psychologist Ron Taffel's book *The Second Family* is subtitled *How Adolescent Power Is Challenging the American Family.*

On the individual level, parents know that one of their most important functions is to teach and model positive values, virtues, and character, and when we cannot do the job alone, we need the support of other adults in the community. One source of guidance on how to do this is Harriet Heath's book *Using Your Values to Raise Your Child to Be an Adult You Admire.* But there is more to it than the one-to-one work of parents with children. There is the school. For information on how schools can help see Thomas Lickona's *Educating for Character: How Our Schools Can Teach Respect and Responsibility.*

So much of our focus throughout this book has been on the

role of individual mindfulness that before concluding we need to say more about social activism. Human beings are social beings as well as spiritual beings. How well we function day to day in the world depends on the quality of our social environment as much as the quality of our spiritual lives. This is particularly true when it comes to preventing the problems of children and youth that concern us so greatly in American society today.

In a report entitled *Running in Place: How American Families Are Faring in a Changing Economy and an Individualistic Society,* sociologist Nicholas Zill and his colleagues at the Westat research center marshal survey data to identify four main challenges facing parents as they seek to encourage good development and character in their teenage offspring. All are themes we have addressed throughout this book.

1. Adult authority is weaker and more fragmented.
2. Young people are spending more time with peers.
3. Teenagers have more freedom in their own lives than previous generations of young people. They have greater freedom of choice regarding friends, school commitments, sexual activity, and career paths.
4. The mass media expose adolescents to a much broader range of experiences, influencing young people in ways that are still under study.

The bottom line, says Zill, is that the peer culture in most American high schools is working against the goals of parents.

A report like Zill's highlights the negative external forces besieging parents. If we open our eyes and use our parent's toolbox, we can see clearly the social toxicity around our children, and the temperamental challenges within. But our culture's fundamental individualism often makes it difficult for us to see the full range of influences that we can draw upon in our com-

munity, culture, and society. As we noted in Chapter 7, one antidote to that narrowly individual focus is to be found in the
work of the Minnesota-based Search Institute.

The Search Institute has put forth a way of looking at the entire social and psychological environment of children in terms
of the presence or absence of a series of assets. Their research
identifies forty such assets. The more children or teenagers
have, the less likely they are to be plagued with problems of violence (assaulting other kids three or more times in the past
twelve months), substance abuse (using illicit drugs such as cocaine, heroin, or amphetamines three or more times in the past
year), and problem alcohol use (using alcohol three or more
times in the past thirty days or getting drunk once or more in
the past two weeks).

With 0 to 10 assets, 61 percent of the kids were in the violent
category; with 31 to 40, only 6 percent. The pattern is much the
same for substance abuse (42 percent with 0 to 10 assets versus
1 percent with 31 to 40) and for problem alcohol use (53 percent with 0 to 10 assets versus 3 percent for 31 to 40). While we
cannot simply conclude that if we provide these assets, kids
will automatically become less violent, less involved in drug or
alcohol use, we can conclude that the more assets kids have in
their lives, the more likely that they will act as we hope they
will act.

This view is consistent with the findings of the Search Institute when it comes to positive behaviors. For school success
(getting mostly A's on the report card), valuing diversity (placing high importance on getting to know people of other races
and ethnic groups), maintaining good health (paying attention
to nutrition and exercise), and delaying gratification (saving
money for something special rather than spending it all right
now), the picture is a mirror image of the problem behaviors:
the more assets kids have, the more positive they are. While
only 7 percent of kids with 0 to 10 assets succeed in school, 53

percent of those with 31 to 40 do. While only 27 percent of those with 0 to 10 assets delay gratification, 72 percent of those with 31 to 40 do.

As we pointed out in Chapter 7, the assets are grouped into eight categories. Here our point is that some assets are under the parents' direct control—for example, "Parent(s) are actively involved in helping young person succeed in school." But other assets are characteristics of the school or community—for example, "School provides a caring, encouraging environment" and "Neighbors take responsibility for monitoring young people's behavior." There is much to be done to support children other than parental actions, and even the parent-oriented assets can benefit from social support.

For example, it is easier to promote "reading for pleasure at least three hours per week" in a community that demonstrates its commitment to literacy via the public library. Getting kids to "spend three or more hours per week in lessons or practice in music, theater, or other arts" is more likely in a community that supports music and art in school and perhaps even has a community school of music and the arts. A 1995 Gallup poll conducted for *Parenting* magazine revealed that 90 percent of parents said they had talked to their children about God. That's a good start, but it is most likely to translate into the asset of "Young person spends one or more hours per week in activities in a religious institution" in a community that is rich with religious institutions and other supports for spiritual practice. These are institutional supports for the assets children need to develop in a positive way. Here is where the parent as citizen comes in.

One of the most important things we can do as parents is support asset-building in the community. How do we do this? It's a matter of who we vote for in local, state, and national government, such as candidates who support the use of public resources to encourage music and the arts for kids. It's a matter of how we spend our time as volunteers, perhaps participating in long-term mentoring projects. It's a matter of carefully choosing the groups to which we contribute money—such as organizations that promote child-abuse prevention and positive parenting. It's a matter of how we behave as members of our community—for example, reaching out to children as neighbors. It's a matter of whether or not we help local government and members of the school board see the need to sponsor and support community-wide character education programs. We need to live our public lives as our highest insights tell us to live within ourselves. As Mahatma Gandhi tells us: "You must be the change you wish to see in the world."

No discussion of this topic would be complete without a strong statement about the gaps in mental health services that fail parents struggling with difficult children and teenagers. The publication of *Lost Boys* in April 1999 elicited a flood of letters, e-mails, and calls from parents around the country who were frantic with worry that their son could be the next school shooter, and who were frustrated to the point of desperation that they could not get effective intervention.

The mother of a troubled, violent 17-year-old wrote:

> My question is, what can we do to get our son help for his problems? Every diagnosis I have tells us he needs a very structured residential home, but nobody wants to pay for it. My husband and I both work full time, but we just can't afford this care. We applied for public assistance to help him and were turned down. So here is a child with above-average intelligence who will probably spend time in jail and be a criminal. We are warning people that he could be dangerous. Nobody seems to want to help. People keep saying, "Look for the signs." Well, our son has all the signs and nobody is listening to us. I do not want to see him locked up but that is what we were advised to do so maybe he can get help. This is

a kid that probably will come out more angry than when he went in, and he's smart enough to figure out how to get revenge. I wish there was more help for people like us. When I heard about what happened in Littleton I thought, "That could be my son." The public really doesn't understand that these kids who commit these terrible crimes are not just normal kids that one day just pick up a gun. These kids are ticking time bombs, and it will happen again. My son has already written a suicide note. My husband and I fear someday he will attack us. Right now he says he hates us. Is anyone in the government listening?

Good question. As a nation, we are in terrible arrears in supporting programs to help lift the siege for parents who live with difficult, troubled children who become dangerous teenagers. If you are wealthy, there are some options—expensive consultants and therapists, solid residential programs. But for other than the wealthy few, there is a desert.

This brings us full circle from where we began in the introduction. Is anyone listening? If not us, who? If not now, when? We hope that every parent reading this book will realize that it is not enough to be a good parent, no matter how daunting that may be to some of us. For our own sakes, to make the world a safer place for our children and all the children we care for, it is important that we look beyond our own families to the communities around us, to the society we inhabit, to the larger family of humanity of which we are all members. And it is vital that we do so with compassion born of understanding.

One final note. We began this book with a promise of humility, compassion, and understanding. We will end there as well. When we sat down with Tom and Sue Klebold in the wake of their son's killing spree and suicide, they asked us for only one thing: that when we were done analyzing, we would help them understand what had happened. In many ways this book is the result of trying to meet that commitment. Does our conceptual toolbox for parents increase our understanding of Dylan and other children who lose their way and drown in the dark side of life? Yes. But does it produce perfect understanding and dispel all mysteries? No. Bad things do happen to good families, good parents, and even good kids. We must accept that.

We don't know everything. We don't understand everything. Our own parenting is far from perfect. We know that, and our kids certainly know that. But if we can all cultivate mindfulness as we analyze and contemplate the imperfections of all families, all parents, all children, we will be ready to move forward—even with our imperfect understanding—as members of a caring community to relieve parents under siege, to replace blame, guilt, and the shame with acceptance, support, and compassion.

Hear the world's great spiritual teachers once more: "You must be the change you wish to see in the world." "Judge not lest ye be judged." "Through universal altruism you develop a feeling of responsibility for others: the wish to actively help them overcome their problems." "Waking up this morning, I smile/Twenty-four brand new hours are before me/I vow to live fully in each moment/and to look at all beings with the eyes of compassion." Wise and compassionate words. Humble words. True words. If we can absorb them and own them in our souls, we will be ready for whatever comes in and from our children, in this moment and the next.

Resources

❧ There are scores of Web sites, magazines, and newsletters devoted to parenting issues. And a visit to the "parenting, child care, and family life" section of a major bookstore reveals hundreds of books on parenting. A visit to Amazon.com reveals nearly 9,000 books catalogued under "parenting." Mostly these are how-to guidance books, such as James Dobson and Gary Bauer's *Children at Risk* (1990), Charlene Giannetti and Margaret Sagarese's *Parenting 911* (1999), Ron Taffel and Melinda Blau's *Nurturing Good Children Now* (1999), Ross Greene's *The Explosive Child* (1998), and Neale Godfrey and Carolina Edwards' *Money Doesn't Grow on Trees: A Parent's Guide to Raising Financially Responsible Children* (1994). Some are "issue" books—e.g., Judith Harris's *The Nurture Assumption* (1998), Michael and Diane Medved's *Saving Childhood* (1999), Dana Mack's *The Assault on Parenthood* (1997), Diane Ehrensaft's *Spoiling Childhood* (1997), and Sylvia Hewlett and Cornel West's *The War Against Parents* (1998). Some even offer a Buddhist spiritual perspective, such as Myla and Jon Kabat-Zinn's *Everyday Blessings: The Inner Work of Mindful Parenting.*

Now that you have read *Parents Under Siege,* you are prepared to make use of these books because now you have a compass to guide you through them. Although we think every parent can find guidance in our book, part of that guidance lies in helping you decide where to go next. *Parents Under Siege* is not the only book a parent needs, but we believe it is a good place to start. For one thing, many of the references will be useful for you as you continue your quest. For example, any parent who faces a temperamentally challenging child would be well advised to read Stanley Greenspan's *The Challenging Child* immediately! If you think that material issues are more pressing, go to Stanley and Danko's *The Millionaire Next Door.* You get the picture.

But there is more. Now that you are oriented, you can pick and choose books to fit your particular set of issues and challenges. From our book you know that assessing context is essential to act wisely and effectively. Most how-to books assume parents can apply a set of rules and actions without regard to analyzing context. *Parents Under Siege* draws out lessons that offer guidance in assessing how to respond to the specifics of your situation, in the social context, the real world, in which you and your children live.

Beyond these books are a host of organizations that provide information, guidance, and support for parents under siege and parents who seek to avoid that fate. On the pages that follow we have identified some that are worth utilizing, and know there are more out there every day.

Organizations

Parents Without Partners

Parents Without Partners is a nonprofit organization for single parents in Canada and the U.S. with over 400 chapters. Under the leadership of volunteer members, local chapters sponsor support meetings and educational activities for single parents. Parents can call (312) 644-6610 for information on the organization or (800) 637-7974 to find a local chapter. For more information, access their Web page at http://www.parentswithoutpartners.org or write to

Parents Without Partners
401 N. Michigan Avenue
Chicago, IL 60611-426

The Fatherhood Project

The Fatherhood Project is a national initiative sponsored by the Families and Work Institute, one of the few organizations that specifically supports fathers. This organization promotes books, films, training programs, and seminars on enhancing fathers' involvement in their children's lives. To learn more about supporting fathers, access the Fatherhood Project Web page at http://www.fatherhoodproject.org or call (212) 465-2044 or write to

The Fatherhood Project
330 7th Avenue, 14th Floor
New York, NY 10001

National Parent Information Network

The National Parent Information Network (NPIN) is a program sponsored by the U.S. Department of Education that provides parents with resources on education, parenting, child care, and child development. NPIN maintains a Web site where parents can obtain information on issues related to children and education. Their "virtual library" contains a listing of numerous books on parenting including summaries and full-text articles. The NPIN web page is available at http://www.npin.org/about.html

Zero to Three: National Center for Infants, Toddlers and Families

Zero to Three is a nonprofit agency that promotes the healthy physical and psychological development of babies and young children. Zero to Three makes research on child development issues available to parents, practitioners, and researchers. The organization also advocates for child-welfare policies, increases public awareness of the importance of the first three years of life, and provides interdisciplinary training and technical assistance to practitioners and researchers on critical issues in the field. For more information on the Zero to Three organization, call (202) 638-1144, access their Web page at http://www.zerotothree.org or write to

Zero to Three
734 15th Street NW, 10th Floor
Washington, DC 20005

The Search Institute

The Search Institute is a nonprofit organization that is dedicated to promoting the healthy development of children and adolescents. The Institute conducts research, promotes programs, and makes research findings available to the public on the well-being of youth. For more information on the Search Institute, including information on their Healthy Communities, Healthy Youth program, and resources on the forty developmental assets referred to in our Epilogue, access their Web page at http://www.search-institute.org or write to

The Search Institute
700 South Third Street, Suite 210
Minneapolis, MN 55415

Communities That Care

Communities That Care (CTC) is a model of community-wide risk and protective factor-focused prevention programs. The CTC "operating system" assists communities in identifying their strengths and areas of need and helps them develop comprehensive, long-range plans and strengthen their existing resources, thereby decreasing risk factors and increasing protective factors for adolescents in their community. CTC also provides training and technical assistance in the development of community-specific programs with clear and measurable outcomes. For more information on Communities That Care, access their Web page at http://www.drp.org/CTC.html or call (800) 736-2630 or write to

Development Research and Programs Inc.
130 Nickerson Street, Suite 107
Seattle, WA 98109

The Center for Media Education

The Center for Media Education (CME) is a nonprofit organization that promotes and provides public education on quality electronic media for children, families, and communities. The Center also conducts research and has been a leader in the promotion of children's educational television programming and safeguards on the Internet. To obtain information on the V-chip, protecting children's privacy on-line, the Children's Television Act (CTA), and other information on family-friendly electronic media, access http://www.cme.org or call (202) 331-7833 or write to

Center for Media Education
2120 L Street, NW, Suite 200
Washington, DC 20037-1527

Game Deputy™ from Deputy Inc.

"Your computer. Your values. Your control" is the motto of Deputy Inc., the creator of the Game Deputy™ computer software program. This software helps parents monitor and restrict their children's use of computer games and maintains a log of when and for how long each game was played. Game Deputy™ displays the Entertainment Software Ratings Board rating and a brief rationale for each game's rating. For example, the rating for *Microsoft NFL Fever 2000* is "Kids to Adults," and the rationale is the game contains "No Violence, No [explicit] Language, No Sexual Content," whereas the rating for the game *Postal* is "Mature (17+)" because the game contains "Blood, Gore, Violence, No [explicit] Language, No Sexual Content." The program is user-friendly, allows parents to set different configurations for each child in the house, and keeps the settings protected under a password set by the parents. Users receive a newsletter each month with information about new games and news related to kids and computer games. Additionally, parents can update their software on-line to include recently released games. The Game Deputy™ software is available on the company's Web site, http://www.deputysoftware.com. The company offers a free trial of the soft-

ware, which can be downloaded from the Web for use on personal comput-
ers. For more information on Game Deputy™, call (214) 359-5342 or write to

Deputy Inc.
4520 Bluffview Boulevard
Dallas, TX 75209

Talking with Kids About Tough Issues

"Talking with Your Kids About Tough Issues" is a national initiative
sponsored by Children Now and the Kaiser Family Foundation. This program encourages parents to talk with their children about violence, sex,
HIV/AIDS, and substance abuse. The organization has created a helpful
Web page at http://www.talkingwithkids.org. Their resources page includes
a list of suggested readings for parents and provides several links to other
helpful sites. To request the "Talking with Your Kids About Tough Issues"
brochure, call (800) CHILD-44.

Warning Signs: A Violence Prevention Guide for Youth

The American Psychological Association and MTV have developed a
Web page entitled "Warning Signs: A Violence Prevention Guide for Youth"
designed to increase awareness of youth violence. Information is provided
on the Web site to help teens and parents recognize some of the warning
signs of youth violence and how to get help for troubled youth. This page is
available at http://helping.apa.org/warningsigns/index.html or call (800)
268-0078 to request a "Warning Signs" brochure.

Educational Consultants

Educational consultants specialize in helping parents select schools and
programs that meet the special needs of their teens. Families are given information about educational opportunities such as finding summer enrichment
programs or selecting a boarding school or college. Consultants can also suggest programs that specialize in working with students with learning disabilities or programs designed for troubled teens, such as wilderness programs or
residential treatment centers. For parents interested in finding therapeutic
placements for their teens with emotional or behavioral problems, it is important to find consultants who have experience working with special-needs students and to inquire about the consultants' training and background in that
field. Parents may also want to find a consultant who not only refers them to a
program but who also monitors the student's progress after placement. George
Posner, Ed. D., is the director of Educational Consulting Services (ECS) and

specializes in working with troubled teens. Parents can access the ECS Web page at *http://www.educationalconsultingservices.com* or e-mail Dr. Posner at *gjp3@cornell.edu*. The Independent Educational Consulting Association (IECA), a nonprofit professional organization of educational advisors, maintains a Web site that includes a national directory of educational consultants. Parents can access this directory on-line at http://www.educationalconsulting.org/ to locate a qualified consultant in their area. Parents can also request information from IECA by calling (703) 591-4850, e-mailing Requests@IECAonline.com or writing to

IECA National Office
3251 Old Lee Highway, Suite 510
Fairfax, Virginia 22030-1504

Family Solutions Program

Family Solutions is an intervention program developed for juvenile offenders and their families by researchers and family therapists. This multifamily group intervention is an alternative to traditional probation or incarceration for first-time offenders, in which the families and the youth attend ten weekly group sessions with other families. The program promotes positive changes in the families' environments by enhancing their communication and coping skills, utilizing their strengths and resources, and altering conflictive cycles of interaction between parents and youth. For more information on the Family Solutions Program, research demonstrating its efficacy, and how to obtain the curriculum for your community, access http://www.fcs.uga.edu/outreach/familysolutions or contact William Quinn, Ph.D., by calling (706) 542-4938, e-mailing bquinn@fcs.uga.edu or writing to

Family Solutions Program
William Quinn, Ph.D.
Department of Child and Family Development
Dawson Hall
University of Georgia
Athens, GA 30602-3622

School-Based Violence Prevention Curricula

The Violence Prevention Curriculum for Adolescents is a program that acknowledges anger as a normal and natural emotion, helps students learn about the risks associated with being involved in violence, and teaches anger management and conflict resolution skills. The Aggressors, Victims, and Bystanders: Thinking and Acting to Prevent Violence curriculum has a slightly larger target audience. The curriculum was designed to help young teens learn how *all* students can play a role in preventing youth violence. The Aggressors, Victims, and Bystanders curriculum shows how victims and bystanders can prevent rather than escalate a fight and how potential aggressors can learn nonaggressive ways of resolving their conflicts. Students participate in small group discussions, role-play real-life scenarios, develop skills for problem solving, and learn alternative ways of negotiating potentially violent situations. Both curricula have been shown effective through evaluation. To learn more about these programs, access their Web page at http://www.edc.org or call (800) 225-4276 or write to

EDC Publishing Center
Millie LeBlanc
Education Development Center, Inc.
55 Chapel Street, Suite 25
Newton, MA 02158-1060

Child Development Media

Child Development Media publishes and distributes videotapes and other materials on a variety of topics of interest to parents and professionals. The organization has an extensive collection of intervention, education, and child-development videotapes and related materials that were developed by child development researchers and professionals. The Child Development Media catalogue includes over 300 titles on topics including prenatal care, learning disabilities, nutrition, temperament, adoption, discipline, divorce, working parents, and violence-prevention programs. Several closed-captioned videos and Spanish titles are also available. The Child Development Media Web page can be accessed at http://www.childdevmedia.com. To request a catalogue, call (800) 405-8942 or write to

Child Development Media
5632 Van Nuys Boulevard, Suite 286
Van Nuys, CA 91401

Children Now

Children Now is a nonprofit organization that supports issues and policies related to child welfare, particularly the welfare of high-risk and impoverished children. Children Now provides information and research on issues such as parenting, child and family health, and child-friendly television and media. Their Web page, available at http://www.childrennow.org

has numerous links to sites on child care, nutrition, working parents, violence prevention, education, and children and the media. To learn more about this organization, call (510) 763-2444 or write to

Children Now
1212 Broadway, 5th Floor
Oakland, CA 94612

Prevent Child Abuse America

Prevent Child Abuse America is a nonprofit organization that works to prevent all types of child abuse and neglect. It conducts research on the prevention of child maltreatment, provides training for prevention programs, and makes resources available to the public on parenting issues. Parents can access the organization's Web page at http://www.preventchildabuse.org to learn more about preventing child abuse and other parenting issues. Their Resources page may be particularly useful for parents because it includes numerous links to other national organizations related to child and family well-being. To learn more about this organization, call (800) CHILDREN or write to

Prevent Child Abuse America
200 S. Michigan Avenue, 17th Floor
Chicago, IL 60604-2404

Child Welfare League of America

The Child Welfare League of America (CWLA) is a nonprofit association of over 1,000 public and nonprofit agencies that provide information and services to families on children's welfare. The association of agencies includes programs on adolescent pregnancy and parenting, adoption, child mental health, substance abuse, juvenile justice, youth development, child maltreatment, and other child-related issues. For information on the CWLA, access their Web page at http://www.cwla.org or call (202) 638-2952 or write to

CWLA Headquarters
440 First Street, NW
Third Floor
Washington, DC 20001-2085

Suggested Readings

And again there are more books.

General Parenting

Beating the Devil Out of Them: Corporal Punishment in American Families (2nd Edition). Murray Straus and Denise Donnelly. New Brunswick, NJ: Transaction, 2001.

Building Healthy Minds: The Six Experiences that Create Intelligence and Emotional Growth in Babies and Young Children. Stanley Greenspan. Cambridge, MA: Perseus, 2000.

The Nurture Assumption: Why Children Turn Out the Way They Do. Judith Harris. New York: Free Press, 1998.

Quick Guide to the Internet for Child Development. Sharon Milburn and Doug Gotthoffer. Boston: Allyn and Bacon, 2000.

Parenting Adolescents

Parenting 911: How to Safeguard and Rescue Your 10- to 15-Year-Old from Substance Abuse, Sexual Encounters . . . and Other Risky Situations. Charlene Giannetti and Margaret Sagarese. New York: Broadway Books, 1999.

Reviving Ophelia: Saving the Selves of Adolescent Girls. Mary Pipher. New York: Grosset/Putnam, 1994.

Surviving Your Adolescents: How to Manage and Let Go of Your 13–18 Year Olds. Thomas Phelan. Glen Ellyn, IL: Child Management Inc., 1998.

A Tribe Apart: A Journey into the Heart of American Adolescence. Patricia Hersch. New York: Ballantine Books, 1999.

Parenting Difficult Children

The Challenging Child: Understanding, Raising and Enjoying the Five "Difficult" Types of Children. Stanley Greenspan. Cambridge, MA: Perseus Books, 1995.

Suggested Readings

The Explosive Child: A New Approach for Understanding and Parenting Easily Frustrated, "Chronically Inflexible" Children. Ross Greene. New York: Harper Collins, 1998.

How to Handle a Hard-to-Handle Kid: A Parent's Guide to Understanding and Changing Problem Behaviors. Drew Edwards. Minneapolis, MN: Free Spirit, 1999.

The Life of a Bipolar Child: What Every Parent and Professional Needs to Know. Trudy Carlson. Duluth, MN: Benline, 2000.

Temperament Talk: A Guide to Understanding Your Child. Kathy Goodman, Lyndall Shick, Barbara Tyler, and Barbara Zukin. La Grande, OR: Center for Human Development, Inc., 1995.

Parenting in Difficult Environments

The Assault on Parenthood: How Our Culture Undermines the Family. Diane Mack. New York: Simon & Schuster, 1997.

Children at Risk: What You Need to Know to Protect Your Family. James Dobson and Gary Bauer. Nashville, TN: Word, 1994.

The New York Times Guide to the Best Children's Videos. New York: Pocket Books, 1999.

The Plug-in Drug: Television, Children, and the Family. Marie Winn. New York: Viking Press, 1985.

Raising Children in a Socially Toxic Environment. James Garbarino. San Francisco: Jossey-Bass, 1995.

Running in Place: How American Families Are Faring in a Changing Economy and an Individualistic Society. Nicholas Zill and Christine Winquist Nord. Washington, DC: Child Trends, 1994.

Saving Childhood: Protecting Our Children from the National Assault on Innocence. Michael Medved and Diane Medved. New York: Harper Perennial, 1999.

Spoiling Childhood: How Well-Meaning Parents Are Giving Children Too Much—But Not What They Need. Diane Ehrensaft. New York: Guilford Press, 1997.

Stop Teaching Our Kids to Kill: A Call to Action Against TV, Movies and Video Game Violence. Dave Grossman and Gloria DeGaetano. New York: Crown, 1999.

The War Against Parents: What We Can Do for America's Beleaguered Moms and Dads. Sylvia Ann Hewlett and Cornel West. Boston, MA: Houghton Mifflin, 1998.

Who's Calling the Shots? How to Respond Effectively to Children's Fasci-

nation with War Play and War Toys. Nancy Carlsson-Paige and Diane Levin. Boston, MA: New Society, 1990.

Spiritual Parenting
Awakening: A Daily Guide to Conscious Living. Shakti Gawain. Novata, CA: New World Library, 1993.

Everyday Blessings: The Inner Work of Mindful Parenting. Myla Kabat-Zinn and Jon Kabat-Zinn. New York: Hyperion, 1998.

Peace Is Every Step: The Path of Mindfulness in Everyday Life. Thich Nhat Hanh. New York: Bantam Books, 1992.

Real Magic: Creating Miracles in Everyday Life. Wayne Dyer. New York: Harper Mass Market Paperbacks, 1993.

10 Principles for Spiritual Parenting: Nurturing Your Child's Soul. Mimi Dce and Marsha Walch. New York: Harper Perennial, 1998.

Character Education and Social Skills
Educating for Character: How Our Schools Can Teach Respect and Responsibility. Thomas Lickona. New York: Bantam Doubleday Dell, 1992.

Emotional Intelligence. Daniel Goleman. New York: Bantam Books, 1997.

High Risk: Children Without a Conscience. Ken Magid and Carole McKelvey. New York: Bantam, 1987.

How Rude! The Teenager's Guide to Good Manners, Proper Behavior, and Not Grossing People Out. Alex Packer. Topeka, KS: Econo-Clad Books, 1999.

The Millionaire Next Door. Thomas Stanley and William Danko. New York: Simon & Schuster, 1999.

Money Doesn't Grow on Trees: A Parent's Guide to Raising Financially Responsible Children. Neale Godfrey and Carolina Edwards. New York: Fireside/Simon & Schuster, 1994.

Nobody Left to Hate: Teaching Compassion After Columbine. Elliot Aronson. New York: W. H. Freeman, 2000.

Nurturing Good Children Now: 10 Basic Skills to Protect and Strengthen Your Child's Core Self. Ron Taffel and Melinda Blau. New York: Golden Books, 1999.

Parents, Kids and Character: 21 Strategies to Help Your Children Develop Good Character. Helen LeGette. Chapel Hill, NC: Character Development Group, 1999.

Raising Cain: Protecting the Emotional Life of Boys. Dan Kindlon and Michael Thomson. New York: Ballantine Books, 2000.

Using Your Values to Raise Your Child to Be an Adult You Admire. Harriet Heath. Seattle, WA: Parenting Press, 2000.

Notes

Preface

xii   And we came to a clearer appreciation: Goleman, D. (1997). *Emotional intelligence.* New York: Bantam Books.

xvi   For example, several studies have shown: Loeber, R., & Farrington, D. (Eds.). (1998). *Serious and violent juvenile offenders: Risk factors and successful interventions.* Thousand Oaks, CA: Sage Publications.

xviii Dylan's picture appeared: Gibbs, N. (1999, May 3). Special Report: The Littleton massacre. *Time,* pp. 20–36.

Chapter 1

3   To paraphrase: Thich Nhat Hanh. (1992). *Peace is every step: The path of mindfulness in everyday life.* New York: Bantam Books.

11   A survey conducted in 1997: Raash, C. (1998, January 5). Optimism grows but citizens disturbed by US political system. *Ithaca Journal.*

12   In 1900 the United States: Adams, H. (1999). *The education of Henry Adams* (1914). Oxford World's Classics. New York: Oxford University Press.

13   All these events: Turner, F. J. (1996). *The frontier in American history* (1897). Mineola, NY: Dover.

14   Some societies: Bronfenbrenner, U. (1970). *Two worlds of childhood: U.S. and U.S.S.R.* New York: Russell Sage Foundation.

14   Today, the United States: Bedard, C. (1996). *Children's rights handbook.* Ithaca, NY: Cornell University and Childhope U.S.A.

18   Boys commit about 85 percent: Garbarino, J. (1999). *Lost boys: Why our sons turn violent and how we can save them.* New York: Free Press.

18   Swedish psychiatrist: Barbro Lunquist, personal communication, February 2000.

19   Research shows: Thomas, A., & Chess, S. (1977). *Temperament and development.* New York: Brunner/Mazel.

19 Psychologists: Loeber, R., & Farrington, D. (Eds.). (1998). *Serious and violent juvenile offenders: Risk factors and successful interventions.* Thousand Oaks, CA: Sage Publications.

19 For example, at the height of: Sloan, J. H., Kellermann, A. L., Reay, D. T., Ferris, J. A., Koepsell, T., Rivara, F. P., Rice, C., Gray, L., and LoGerfo, J. (1988). Handgun regulations, crime, assaults, and homicide: A tale of two cities. *New England Journal of Medicine, 319*(19), 1256–1262.

20 In the mid-1970s: Achenbach, T., & Howell, C. (1993). Are American children's problems getting worse? A thirteen-year comparison. *Journal of the American Academy of Child and Adolescent Psychiatry, 32*(6), 1145–1154.

21 For example, in the wake of: Kirk, M., Connor, K., & Navasky, M. (Producers) (2000). The killer at Thurston High [Documentary]. Available from Frontline:
http://www.pbs.org/wgbh/pages/frontline/programs/categories/c.html

21 Truman Capote: Capote, T. (1992). *In cold blood: A true account of a multiple murder and its consequences.* New York: Modern Library.

21 When *The New York Times:* Fessenden, F. (2000, April 9). How youngest killers differ: Peer support. *New York Times,* p. 29.

Chapter 2

25 For example, an article: Schrofus, J. (May 17, 1999). Who's guilty: Parents are being sued and jailed for their children's sins. *U.S. News & World Report.*

25 Some 44,000 children: U.S. Department of Health and Human Services Children's Bureau. (January 2000). *The adoption and foster care analysis and reporting system (AFCARS) report* [On-line]. Available: http://www.acf.dhhs.gov/programs/cb

26 The effects are usually: Collins, A., Maccoby, E., Steinberg, L., Hetherington, E., & Bornstein, M. (2000). Contemporary research on parenting: The case for nature and nurture. *American Psychologist, 55*(2), 218–232.

26 For example, a study: Bohman, M. (1996). Predisposition to criminality: Swedish adoption studies in retrospect. In G. R. Bock & J. A. Goode (Eds.), *Genetics of criminal and antisocial behavior, Ciba Foundation Symposium 194* (pp. 99–114). Chichester, England: Wiley.

27 When these children were adopted: Ibid.

28 In October 2000: Murkoff, H. (2000, Fall/Winter). The real parenting expert is . . . you. *Newsweek,* pp. 20–21.

28 As the author, Heidi Murkoff: Ibid.

28 In an article. Hertzberg, H. (1999, July 26). The parent trap: How did they ever raise kids without magazines? *The New Yorker,* pp. 91–93.

29 Cornell University psychologists: Williams, W., & Ceci, S. (1998). *Escaping the advice trap: 59 tough relationship problems solved by the experts.* Kansas City: Andrews McMeel Publishing.

32 After reviewing all the evidence: Bruer, J. (1999). *The myth of the first three years: A new understanding of early brain development and lifelong learning.* New York: Free Press.

32 Thus, for example: Bronfenbrenner, U. (1972). *Influences on human development.* Hinsdale, IL: Dryden Press.

32 And according to the research: Loeber, R., & Farrington, D. (Eds.). (1998). *Serious and violent juvenile offenders: Risk factors and successful interventions.* Thousand Oaks, CA: Sage Publications.

33 According to the classic research: Thomas, A., & Chess, S. (1977). *Temperament and development.* New York: Brunner/Mazel.

34 A survey conducted by the Gannett: Raash, C. (1998, January 5). Optimism grows but citizens disturbed by US political system. *Ithaca Journal.*

36 In a study: Sameroff, A., Seifer, R. Barocas, R., Zax, M., & Greenspan, S. (1987). Intelligence quotient scores of 4-year-old children: Social environment risk factors. *Pediatrics, 79,* 343–350.

37 Research conducted: Perry, B. D., Pollard, R. A., Blakley, T. L., Baker, W. L, & Vigilante, D. (1995). Childhood trauma, the neurobiology of adaptation, and "use-dependent" development of the brain: How "states" become "traits." *Infant Mental Health Journal, 16*(4), 271–291.

37 What is more: Tolan, P., & Henry, D. (1996). Patterns of psychopathology among urban poor children: Comorbidity and aggression. *Journal of Consulting and Clinical Psychology, 64*(5), 1094–1099.

40 The famous psychoanalyst: Erikson, E. H. (1963). *Childhood and society* (2nd Ed.). New York: Norton.

41 The term *social toxicity:* Garbarino, J. (1995). *Raising children in a socially toxic environment.* San Francisco, CA: Jossey-Bass.

Chapter 3

56 Researchers: Loeber, R., & Farrington, D. (Eds.). (1998). *Serious and violent juvenile offenders: Risk factors and successful interventions.* Thousand Oaks, CA: Sage Publications.

57 Autism, too, is linked: Cowley, G., Foote, D., & Tesoriero, H. (July 31, 2000). Understanding autism. *Newsweek.*

57 A study by Harvard psychologist: Caspi, A., Elder, G. H., & Bem, D. J. (1987). Moving against the world: Life-course patterns of explosive children. *Developmental Psychology, 23*(2), 308–313.

59 Psychologist Lewis Lipsitt: Lipsitt, L. (1999, July). Anger springs from complex combination of traits. *Brown University Child and Adolescent Behavior Letter, 15*(7), 1–4.

59 The classic research: Patterson, G. (1982). *Coercive family process.* Eugene, OR: Castalia.

60 Decades of research: Bowlby, J. (1982). Attachment and loss: Retrospect and prospect. *American Journal of Orthopsychiatry, 52*(4), 664–678.

64 Patterson's lessons: Patterson, G. (1982). *Coercive family process.* Eugene, OR: Castalia.

64 Research shows: Wilson, S. J., & Lipsey, M. W. (2000). Wilderness challenge programs for delinquent youth: A meta-analysis of outcome evaluations. *Evaluation and Program Planning, 23*, 1–12.

64 One "yes" comes from: Achenbach, T., & Howell, C. (1993). Are American children's problems getting worse? A thirteen-year comparison. *Journal of the American Academy of Child and Adolescent Psychiatry, 32*(6), 1145–1154.

67 We will discuss television: Maccoby, E. (1951). Television: Its impact on school children. *Public Opinion Quarterly, 15*, 421–444.

69 One is tempted to conclude: Bahr, H. (1980). Changes in family life in Middletown, 1924–1977. *Public Opinion Quarterly, 44*, 35–52.

71 In 1970, 53 percent of the women: Garbarino, J. (1995). *Raising children in a socially toxic environment.* San Francisco, CA:Jossey-Bass.

Chapter 4

79 Research conducted by sociologists: Carlson, B. E. (1984). Children's observations of interparental violence, In A. R. Roberts (Ed.), *Battered women and their families* (pp. 147–167) New York: Springer. Status, M. (1992). Children as witnesses to marital violence: A risk factor for lifelong problems among a nationally representative sample of American men and women. In D. F. Schwarz (Ed.), *Children and violence, Report of the 23 Ross Roundtable on Critical Approaches to Common Pediatric Problems* (pp. 98–109). Columbus, OH: Ross Laboratories.

79 What is more: National Center on Child Abuse and Neglect. (1996). *The third national incidence study of child abuse and neglect (NIS-3).* Washington, D.C.: U.S. Department of Health and Human Services.

79 A third of the children: Schwab-Stone M. E., Ayers, T. S., Kasprow, W., Voyce, C., Barone, C., Shriver, T.,& Weissberg, R. P. (1995). No safe haven: A study of violence exposure in an urban community. *Journal of the American Academy of Child and Adolescent Psychiatry, 34*(10), 1343–1352.

80 A national survey: Ingrassia, M. (1993, November 22). Growing up fast and frightened. *Newsweek.*

80 A Harris poll: Garbarino, J. (1999). *Lost boys: Why our sons turn violent and how we can save them.* New York: Free Press.

80 In 1999: *New York Times* (1999, October).

80 A study conducted by pediatricians: Price, J.,& Desmond, S. (1987). The missing children issue: A preliminary examination of 5th grade students' perceptions. *American Journal of Diseases of Children, 141,* 811–815.

84 Our reference is: Heller, J. (1961). *Catch-22.* New York: Simon & Schuster.

88 A research group: Hubbs, T., Laura, Hughes, K. P., Culp, A. M., Osofsky, J. D., Hann, D. M., Alice, E. W., & Ware, L. M. (1996). Children of adolescent mothers: Attachment representation, maternal depression, and later behavior problems. *American Journal of Orthopsychiatry, 66*(3), 416–426.

90 The reference here is: Milgram, S. (1974). *Obedience to authority.* New York: Harper & Row.

93 Child psychiatrist: Terr, L. (1981). Psychic trauma in children: Observations following the Chowchilla school-bus kidnapping. *American Journal of Psychiatry, 138*(1), 14–19.

93 Research gathered by the National Research Council: Reiss, A. J., & Rothe, J. A. (Eds.). (1993). *Understanding and preventing violence.* Washington, D.C.: National Academy Press.

93 Psychologist Leonard Eron: Huesmann, L. R., Eron, L. D., Lefkowitz, M. M., & Walder, L. O. (1984). Stability of aggression over time and generations. *Developmental Psychology, 20*(6), 1120–1134.

94 Psychologist Stephen Asher: Erdley, C. A., & Asher, S. (1998). Linkages between children's beliefs about the legitimacy of aggression and their behavior. *Social Development, 7*(3), 321–339.

95 A *New York Times:* Fessenden, F. (2000, April 9). How youngest killers differ: Peer support. *New York Times,* p. 29.

95 At its worst: American Psychiatric Association. (1994). *Diagnostic and statistical manual of mental disorders (4ᵗʰ ed.).* Washington, D.C.: Author.

96 Psychologist Nick Stennet: Stennet, N. (1983). Family relationships and school achievement among boys of lower-income urban black families. *American Journal of Orthopsychiatry, 53*(1), 127–143.

96 Anthropologist Dan Sheinfeld: Sheinfeld, D. (1983). Family relationships and school achievement among boys of lower income urban black families. *American Journal of Orthopsychiatry, 53*(1), 127–143.

Chapter 5

98 In their important: Ceci, S. J., & Bruck, M. (1995). *Jeopardy in the courtroom: A scientific analysis of children's testimony.* Washington, D.C.: American Psychological Association.

98 Even in the early decades: Piaget, J. (1952). *The origins of intelligence in children.* New York: International Universities Press.

100 Psychologist Peter Crabb: Crabb, P. (2000). The material culture of homicidal fantasies. *Aggressive Behavior 26*(3), 225–234.

106 Results of a recent study by Swedish psychologists: Kerr, M., & Stattin, H. What parents know, how they know it, and several forms of adolescent adjustment: Further support for a reinterpretation of monitoring. *Developmental Psychology, 36*(3), 366–380.

108 As documented: Brownlee, S. (1999, August 9). Inside the teen brain. *U.S. News & World Report.*

109 As reported in *Time* magazine: Gibbs, N & Roche, T. (1999, December 20). The Columbine tapes. *Time.*

111 Social psychologists call this the *fundamental attribution error:* Ross, L. (1977). The intuitive psychologist and his shortcomings: Distortions in the attribution process. In L. Berkowitz (Ed.), *Advances in experimental psychology* (Vol. 10). New York: Academic Press.

111 Writing in *Time* magazine: Dickenson, A. (1999, May 3). Where were the parents? *Time,* p. 40.

112 The documentary about Kip Kinkel: Kirk, M., Connor, K., & Navasky, M. (Producers) (2000). The killer at Thurston High [Documentary]. Available from Frontline:
http://www.pbs.org/wgbh/pages/frontline/programs/categories/c.html

Chapter 6

125 Psychologist: Bronfenbrenner, U. (1970). *Two worlds of childhood: U.S. and U.S.S.R.* New York: Russell Sage Foundation.

126 Psychoanalyst: Bettelheim, B., & Rosenfeld, A. (1993). *The art of the obvious: Developing insight for psychotherapy and everyday life.* New York: Knopf.

126   In *The Boy Who Would Be a Helicopter:* Paley, Vivian. (1990). *The boy who would be a helicopter.* Cambridge, MA: Harvard University Press.

129   Evidence on the effectiveness: Wilson, S. J., & Lipsey, M. W. (2000). Wilderness challenge programs for delinquent youth: A meta-analysis of outcome evaluations. *Evaluation and Program Planning, 23,* 1–12.

135   There are physiological reasons: Kranowitz, C. (1998). *The out-of-sync child: Recognizing and coping with sensory integration dysfunction.* New York: Perigee.

141   As the Zen master: Thich Nhat Hanh. (1992). *Peace is every step: The path of mindfulness in everyday life.* New York: Bantam Books.

142   In her book: Aron, E. (1999). *The highly sensitive person: How to thrive when the world overwhelms you.* New York: Broadway Books.

144   Psychologist Daniel Goleman: Goleman, D. (1997). *Emotional intelligence.* New York: Bantam Books.

144   A quarter of a century ago: Rohner, R. (1975). *They love me, they love me not: A worldwide study of the effects of parental acceptance and rejection.* New Haven, CT: HRAF Press.

145   Remember that: Thomas, A., & Chess, S. (1977). *Temperament and development.* New York: Brunner/Mazel.

147   The Russian psychologist: Vygotsky, L. (1978). *Mind in society: The development of higher psychological processes.* Cambridge, MA: Harvard University Press.

Chapter 7
151   Reading Tom Brokaw's: Brokaw, T. (1998). *The greatest generation.* New York: Random House.

152   The National Survey of Youth: Garbarino, J. (1995). *Raising children in a socially toxic environment.* San Francisco, CA: Jossey-Bass.

152   In 1963: Ibid.

154   In his book: Moore, T. (1993). *Care of the soul: A guide for cultivating depth and sacredness in everyday life.* New York: Harper Collins.

156   There are kids who need help: Zito, J. M., Safer, D., dosReis, S., Gardner, J. F., Boles, M., & Lynch, F. (2000). Trends in the prescribing of psychotropic medications to preschoolers. *Journal of the American Medical Association, 283*(8).

157   That is not to say: Shute, N., Locy, T., & Pasternak, D. (2000, March 6) The perils of pills: The psychiatric medication of children is dangerously haphazard. *U.S. News & World Report,* pp. 44–50.

159   This research: Barker, R., & Gump, P. (1964). *Big school, small school:*

High school size and student behavior. Stanford, CA: Stanford University Press.

161 Psychologist Rudolf Moos: Nielsen, H. D, & Moos, R. H. (1977). Student-environment interaction in the development of physical symptoms. *Research in Higher Education, 6*(2), 139–156.

162 Educational psychologist: deLara, E. (2000). *Adolescents' perceptions of safety at school and their solutions for enhancing safety and decreasing school violence: A rural case study.* Unpublished doctoral dissertation, Cornell University, Ithaca, NY.

163 One of the leaders in this approach: Scales, P. C., & Leffert, N. (1999). *Developmental assets: A synthesis of scientific research on adolescent development.* Minneapolis, MN: Search Institute.

165 Reading accounts: Krajicek, D. (2000, January 2). *New York Times.* Krajicek, D. (1999, November). Boot camps lose early swagger. *Youth Today, 8*(10), 17, 33, 35.

166 Thus, for example: Symonds, P. (1949). *The dynamics of parent-child relationships.* New York: Bureau of Publications, Teachers College, Columbia University.

166 But a study of permissive child rearing: Baumrind, D. (1971). Current patterns of parental authority. *Developmental Psychology Monograph, 4* (No. 1, Part 2), 1–103.

166 Research conducted by psychologist Al Baldwin: Baldwin, A., Baldwin, C., & Cole, R. (1990). Stress-resistant families and stress-resistant children. In J. Rolf (Ed.), *Risk and protective factors in the development of psychopathology.* New York: Cambridge University Press.

169 Research in the United States: Gibbs, J. & Huange, L. (Eds.). (1997). *Children of color: Psychological interventions with culturally diverse youth.* San Francisco, CA: Jossey-Bass.

Chapter 8

175 James McNeal: McNeal, J. *The kids market: Myths and realities.* New York: Paramount Market Publishing.

175 Writing in *Mothering Magazine:* Ruskin, G. Why they whine. *Mothering Magazine* [On-line] Available: http://www.mothering.com/SpecialArticles/Issue97/whine.htm

175 This is business as usual: Clay, R. (2000). Advertising to children: Is it ethical? *Monitor on Psychology, 31*(8), 52–53.

178 In 1950: Bureau of Labor Statistics. (June 19, 2000). Labor force sta-

tistics from the Current Population Survey. Employment status of parents. [On-line]. Available:
http://stats.bls.gov/news.release/famee.t04.htm

187 Joe Dominguez: Dominguez, J., & Robin, V. (1999). *Your money or your life: Transforming your relationship with money and achieving financial independence.* New York: Penguin.

Chapter 9

190 As early as 1936: Pear, T. H. (1936). What television might do. *Listener, 18.*

190 By 1972, a report to the Surgeon General: American Psychological Association. (1993). *Summary report of the American Psychological Association commission on Violence and youth: Vol. I. Violence and youth: Psychology's response.* Washington, D.C.: Author.

191 The American Psychological Association: Ibid.

192 Developmental psychologist: Maccoby, E. (1951). Television: Its impact on school children. *Public Opinion Quarterly, 15,* 421–444.

192 A study conducted: Hamilton, R., & Lawless, R. (1956). Television within the social matrix. *Public Opinion Quarterly, 20*(2), 393–403.

193 Other studies found: Ibid.

194 In her 1998 book: Cantor, J. (1998). *Mommy, I'm scared: How TV and movies frighten children.* New York: Harcount Brace.

196 Schools can help: Pedersen, D., Wingert, P., Weingarten, T., Cooper, A., Gesalman, A., & Getland, L. (2000, July 3). Generation XXL. *Newsweek,* pp. 40–44.

197 From 1964 to 1994: Ibid.

197 In the South Pacific: Becker, A. (1999, May 20). *Sharp rise in eating disorders in Fiji follows arrival of TV.* Retrieved March 29, 2001 from Harvard Medical School Office of Public Affairs:
http://www.hms.harvard.edu/news/releases/599bodyimage.html

199 For example, a study: Hallowell, E. (1999). *Connect.* New York: Pantheon Books.

201 Shortly after the Columbine shootings: Harmon, A. (1999, April 24). These song on the Internet: The pain of social ostracism. *New York Times,* p. A12.

201 In World War II: Grossman, D., & Kloske, G. (1996). *On killing: The psychological cost of learning to kill in war and society.* New York: Little Brown & Co.

202 One study found that: Funk, J., & Buchman, D. (1996). Playing violent

video and computer games and adolescent self concept. *Journal of Communication, 46*(2), 19–33.

203   Paul Lynch and his colleagues: Lynch, P. J. (1999). Hostility, Type A behavior, and stress hormones at-rest and after playing violent video games in teenagers. *Psychosomatic Medicine, 61,* 113.

203   Craig Anderson: Anderson, C., & Dill, K. (2000). *Journal of Personality and Social Psychology, 78*(4), 772–790.

Epilogue

205   Thus, psychologist: Taffel, R. (2001). *The second family: How adolescent power is challenging the American family.* New York: St. Martin's Press.

207   The Search Institute: Scales, P. C., & Leffert, N. (1999). *Developmental assets: A synthesis of scientific research on adolescent development.* Minneapolis, MN: Search Institute.

208   A 1995 Gallop Poll: Brown, H. (2000, December/January). The search for spirituality. *Parenting,* pp. 114–119.

Index